KIDSOURCE

MAGIC TRICKS

By Shawn McMaster
Illustrated by Mike Moran

LOWELL HOUSE JUVENILE
LOS ANGELES
NTC/Contemporary Publishing Group

This book is for Martin Gardner, and to the memory of Walter B. Gibson and Bill Severn—whose extraordinary magic books fed my interest as a young boy, for which I am very grateful today.

—S.M.

Published by Lowell House
A division of NTC/Contemporary Publishing Group, Inc.
4255 West Touhy Avenue, Lincolnwood (Chicago), Illinois 60712 U.S.A.

Managing Director and Publisher: Jack Artenstein
Director of Publishing Services: Rena Copperman
Editorial Director: Brenda Pope-Ostrow
Project Editor: Joanna Siebert
Designer: Treesha Runnells Vaux

Lowell House books can be purchased at special discounts when ordered in bulk for premiums and special sales. Contact Customer Service at the address above, or call 1-800-323-4900.

Printed and bound in the United States of America

Library of Congress Catalog Card Number: 99-73106

ISBN: 0-7373-0231-3

DHD 10 9 8 7 6 5 4 3 2 1

CONTENTS

ACKNOWLEDGMENTS

I would like to take this opportunity to thank a number of people who, in one form or another, helped in the creation of this book. Thank you to Jim Starr, Jeff Semel, Christopher Hart, Johnny Ace Palmer, Susan Wiltfang, Brian Flora, David Byron, Stephen Minch, and Ron Wilson. Thank you also to my editor at Lowell House, Joanna Siebert, for being helpful, but more important, patient and understanding.

Special thanks to Amy Downing, formerly of Lowell House, for giving me back the writing bug at a time when I was able to take it back. *All* of my writing projects since I began again in 1995 have been possible because of the inspiration and confidence gained after that first project with Amy as editor.

Thanks should also go to David and Suzan Gullett for their initial hand in this whole scheme of things.

Last, but not least, my family should be thanked for putting up with the time and various moods they had to endure while I was writing. Theresa, Hannah, and Peri: I love you very much.

INTRODUCTION

If you have ever seen a magician perform, you know what an amazing experience it can be—coins appearing from nowhere, elephants vanishing, and ladies floating in midair! You may have walked away from a magic performance wondering, "How did they do that?" Well, now's your chance to find out!

You are about to become a magician! And *KidSource: Magic Tricks* will help. You will learn a little about the history of this mysterious art through fascinating stories about some of the tricks and magicians of long ago. You will be let in on some basic information that all magicians must remember when performing their tricks.

Next, a whole world of magic tricks is opened up for you! You will learn tricks with cards and coins, tricks using things you can find in any home, mind-reading tricks, and daring escapes! You will not have to hunt down any special magic props to accomplish these marvelous mysteries.

Once you have mastered the tricks, *KidSource: Magic Tricks* will help you put them all together into an act that you can perform for audiences of all ages. When your show is over, you can take in a magic show yourself. *KidSource: Magic Tricks* contains a chapter listing some of the places around the country where you can see a live magic show.

If you want to mystify people further, there is a list of magic shops, books, and magazines that will assist you in learning more about the art of magic. There is even a special glossary of magic terms at the back of the book. *KidSource: Magic Tricks* provides absolutely everything you need to know about performing magic. So read on and have fun!

A HISTORY OF HOCUS-POCUS

"A magician is an actor playing the part of a magician."

—Jean Eugène Robert-Houdin, French magician (1805–1871)

Chances are, you've seen a magician perform. It might have been at a birthday party or at your school. Maybe a magician came by your table at a restaurant where you sat with your family. Maybe you've seen one on television. Regardless of where or when, you were probably amazed at the feats performed before your eyes and most likely wondered, "How did he do that?" Many people wonder that, but not too many stop to think *Why does he do that?*

What makes magicians want to fool people? How *did* magic begin?

The word *magic* can be traced back to the ancient Greeks and Romans and their word *magia,* used to describe **occult** knowledge and practices of Persian magicians. Even so, we do not know for sure who performed the first magic trick. There is evidence that some of the tricks performed by magicians today have been around since before the time of Moses, and a few tricks, such as the Cups and Balls and Chinese Linking Rings, are so ancient that their origins are untraceable.

Some believe that magic was first used by human beings as a way of deceiving others and gaining power and wealth. Others believe that magic was used early on by individuals called "shamans," or "medicine men/women" as a way of healing the sick and giving hope to suffering people.

In any case, the first recorded magic performance, done as pure entertainment, was by a magician named Dedi in the Egyptian pharaoh Cheops's court over 3,000 years ago. Dedi's tricks included cutting off the head of a chicken and then magically restoring it. Dedi was also said to have caused a fierce lion to follow him around as if it were a harmless kitten.

In the 15th century, when the Inquisition held sway in parts of Europe, anyone caught doing anything even resembling magic was labeled a witch and put to death. People who performed simple **sleight of hand** were charged with practicing witchcraft and therefore killed.

After having long been considered a less than respectable entertainment —if not a downright evil—magic finally began to emerge in a more favorable light by the end of the 18th century. By this time, drawing-room entertainers, magicians among them, had become popular. Beginning in the 19th century, magic could be seen in many of the music halls and variety theaters that were springing up around the world.

Creature Features!

During the 1930s and 1940s, and even into the 1950s, a different kind of magic show became very popular with teenagers. It was called the "Spook Show." These shows—with names like Zombie Jamboree, Midnight Voodoo Party, and Dr. Silkini's Asylum of Horrors—usually took place at midnight at a local movie house.

A magician would present a show usually incorporating some "spooky" themes. Slowly building eerie anticipation in the audience, he or she would conjure up a collection of monsters and ghouls. They would charge from the stage toward the audience and, just then, the lights would go out! Ghosts (actually bits of sheet on string) flew around the theater. There was pandemonium. People screamed.

When the magician felt they'd had enough, the lights would come back up long enough for him or her to thank the audience and introduce the movie that was about to start.

These theaters thrived for years offering vaudeville shows that featured variety acts, or performances of all kinds, on stage. Magicians played these vaudeville circuits, and during the early 1900s large traveling magic shows toured the world as well. All throughout Europe and America, and even in Australia and parts of Asia, big-name magicians performed full-evening shows complete with lavish musical numbers and elaborate costumes. Each show usually featured a number of special **illusions** made popular by these magicians for which the public clamored. Among the magicians offering these grand performances were Harry Blackstone, Chung Ling Soo, Howard Thurston, Harry Kellar, and Harry Houdini.

Magic continued its popularity into the 1940s during the golden age of radio. Who would think that magic could be performed over the radio? But a man named Joseph Dunninger did just that. He had a highly rated radio show featuring his special brand of magic called **"mentalism."**

Motion pictures had already become popular, and in the 1950s television entered the scene. Because of this, more and more variety theaters closed down, and large-scale magic productions became a thing of the past. Some magicians, however, began designing shows that could play in movie houses either before the movie or between pictures. Many of these shows were performed before the screening of a scary monster movie and so were known as "Spook Shows." Tricks performed in dim light were presented in other "spooky" ways, too. At the end of the show, just as the lights in the theater were going out, people dressed in monster costumes would often leap out into the audience from the stage. Imagine the screaming that went on in *those* shows!

Don't Burn That Witch Until You've Read This Book!

In 1584 the first magic book written in English was published in London. Called *The Discoverie of Witchcraft,* it was written by Reginald Scot. Along with describing spells and natural remedies for various illnesses, the book reveals the secrets of how to perform magic tricks of the time. Early versions of many of the tricks performed by today's magicians can be found in the pages of Scot's book.

Interestingly, Scot did not print the secrets to the tricks to harm magicians but to help them. Scot was so outraged over the church of that era's practice of witch-hunting and execution, he sought to inform the public that what they believed was witchcraft was something very different. Scot's book was reprinted a second and third time, but after the turn of the century, King James I ordered it burned.

In the 1950s, magic made its entrance into television. In 1960, Mark Wilson became the first magician to present a weekly magic series on national television. It was called *The Magic Land of Allakazam* and featured Wilson and the cast performing different exciting illusions each week. Wilson, who went on to produce many other successful magic programs for television, taught actor Bill Bixby all of the magic he performed in his 1970s television series, *The Magician.*

Today, magic is enjoying renewed interest and popularity. Unfortunately, not many traveling magic shows equal the ones presented earlier in this century. Perhaps the only one currently on the road that is even close is David Copperfield's. His fast-paced and elaborate show features a mixture of magic styles. The magic team of Siegfried and Roy specializes in spectacle, too—complete with fire-breathing dragon! Their show does not travel, however. If you want to see it, *you* will have to travel: to Las Vegas, Nevada.

PERFORMER PROFILE: CHUNG LING WHO?

One of the more interesting magicians touring during the early 1900s was Chung Ling Soo. Despite his name and appearance onstage, Chung Ling Soo wasn't Asian at all. His real name was William Ellsworth Robinson and he was born in New York. Sound confusing? Robinson admired a real Asian performer named Ching Ling Foo. In 1898, Ching Ling Foo was the rage in Europe and America. An agent offered Robinson work if he could perform an act like Ching Ling Foo's. Robinson, grabbing the opportunity, created a Chinese stage character named Chung Ling Soo and began performing in England and France. He gradually changed his act, adding more original material, and eventually became more popular than Ching Ling Foo himself! Soon Robinson began acting the part of Chung Ling Soo offstage as well as on. He even gave interviews through a "Chinese interpreter." Chung Ling Soo died onstage in 1918 while attempting his most famous and dramatic trick: the Bullet Catch. His assistants would fire guns, one of them containing a marked bullet, at Chung Ling Soo, and he would catch the bullet in his teeth. On this night, however, due to a malfunction in the special gun used for the trick, Chung Ling Soo was shot dead.

Robert-Houdin was an ingenious magician and scientist. Today he is considered the "father of modern magic." It was Robert-Houdin who, dressed in formal wear, brought magic off the streets and into the parlors of wealthy dignitaries. Because of Robert-Houdin, magic gained respect and acceptance as a performing art.

Faced with the problem of the Algerian warriors, Robert-Houdin devised a clever trick. Holding a small wooden chest, he met with the warriors. Simple in appearance, the chest had a handle on the top. Robert-Houdin told the warriors he would rob them of their strength. To prove he had indeed done so, he asked a child to lift the chest. Once the child had lifted and set the chest back down, he invited any of the warriors to lift it as well. *None of them could!* This caused them great anxiety and fear. A small child could lift the chest, yet they could not! The Algerians finally surrendered, figuring they were no match against French magic.

The Magic Trick That Won a War

In 1856, Napoleon III was faced with a group of Algerian warriors rebelling against French rule. The warriors, mighty in number *and* reputation, claimed to have the power of magic on their side—and this magic would help them win their independence. Deciding to fight magic with magic, Napoleon turned to France's greatest magician: Jean Eugène Robert-Houdin.

GETTING STARTED—
THINGS YOU SHOULD KNOW BEFORE OPENING YOUR BAG OF TRICKS

"The end of all magic is to feed with mystery the human mind, which dearly loves mystery."

—Harry Kellar (1849–1922), professional magician

So how does one go about becoming a magician anyway? What does it take? Is all you need a top hat and a rabbit? Does it take years and years of practice, or can you master a magic trick in just a day or so? Do you need big boxes and flashy costumes? Do you need lots of money?

Well . . . yes and no.
Let's begin with *you*.

MAKE YOURSELF PRESENTABLE

Magic is a performance art. That means you're going to be seen. Seen by *many* people. And, unlike much performance art—for example, playing with a symphony orchestra—where the performer has some distance from the audience, many times in magic you are interacting with your audience. You may ask for someone to come join you on stage, or you may be sitting or standing at a table with a group of people. Whatever the situation, you must look your best. First impressions count. If you make your entrance on stage right after lunch with a piece of lettuce between your teeth, the impact of that first impression is lost! Remember, your clothes and your appearance are just as important as any magical prop.

HANDS

Take a good look at your hands. Are they clean? Is there dirt under your nails? Do the nails need trimming, or are they ragged from being bitten? Is the skin on your hands rough or smooth?

A magician's hands are his most important tools. Because the audience will tend to focus on them during a performance, they must be properly taken care of. So, regularly trim and file your nails. And keep your hands clean at all times, as well as smooth and supple-looking.

BASIC GROOMING

Make sure that your hair is washed and neatly combed. And brush your teeth! Remember that you will be interacting with members of your audience. Some of the time they may be very close to you, possibly even standing right next to you. Do them a favor and be sure your teeth are brushed and your breath smells pleasant. Use a mouth-wash if necessary.

KIDSOURCE TIPS

It is very important that your hands stay looking their best. If you have a problem with dry skin (and even if you don't), a good hand lotion used regularly will keep your hands looking smooth. Try to find a lotion that absorbs quickly into the skin and is not greasy. Try out a few brands until you find one that is right for you.

CLOTHES

The type of clothes you wear to perform in will depend on a number of things, including the character—if any—you will be portraying, the location where you will be performing, and the type of show you will be presenting. Whatever style of clothes you wear, however, they should be neat and clean. Clothing that is wrinkled, dirty, or full of holes will not make a good impression on your audience.

If you are performing as a character of some sort, make sure your costume has enough pockets to store your props. Characters such as traveling street performers or jesters may carry pouches or bags that contain their props.

If you are not performing as a character, an elaborate costume is probably out of place. Boys should consider wearing a nice dress shirt and matching tie. Add a sport jacket or coat, and you not only have spiffed up your outfit, but you have also increased your pocket space for props and supplies. For girls, a smart-looking pants outfit or dress work fine.

Whatever their style, if your clothes are neat and tidy you will feel better about yourself, and that confidence will come across when performing your magic. Audiences will find your performance irresistible. You will gain command of them and of your show right from the start.

WHO WILL YOU BE WHEN PERFORMING?

You will be performing your magic in front of lots of people. Let your imagination run wild and create a character to add to the appeal of your performances. Will you be a magic clown? An ancient wizard? A serious-looking master illusionist in tuxedo and top hat? Or will you just be yourself? That's OK, too.

Your character may not come to you right away. In fact, sometimes you may not be able to decide on a character until you discover what type of magic you enjoy performing. So keep an open mind, and think about the type of stage persona you want to convey.

THE TWO MOST IMPORTANT RULES OF MAGIC

There are two very important rules that, as a magician, you must always keep in mind. All magicians follow these rules, and if you follow them yourself it will make your tricks and your persona as a magician much more powerful.

The number one rule of magic is *Never reveal the secrets to your tricks*. Whenever you perform a magic trick, you are creating a sense of wonder in the minds of your audience. If you were to follow up the trick by explaining how it was done, not only would you be robbing your audience of that sense of wonder, but you would also risk reducing the trick in their eyes to a mere puzzle or even a joke. Plus, by reducing the impact of the trick, you also lessen the importance of what *you* do as a magician. People will stop thinking of you as a person capable of creating mysteries and begin considering you a mere prankster.

Bottom line: If you can't keep a secret, don't perform magic! Close this book right now!

Are you still here? Good. Let's continue . . .

As with most rules, there is an exception to this one. Many top magicians would not be where they are today had it not been for the mentoring of other magicians. Who better to learn magic from than another magician? That means sharing secrets. The *only* person you can reveal a magic secret to, then, is another magician.

The second important rule to remember is ***Never repeat a trick for the same audience.*** No matter how much they plead with you, don't allow yourself to be pressured into repeating a trick or you run the risk of its secret being revealed.

The first time you perform a magic trick, you take your audience by surprise. They were not expecting to see what they just did. But if you were to perform that same trick again, your audience would not be watching it the same way. Instead, they would be watching *every move you made*!

Are there exceptions to *this* rule?

Yes.

First, only repeat a trick if you know *another* way of doing it. That way, you will still throw your audience off. It will take them a few moments to refocus. That's all the time you need to fool them all over again! By the time they realize you are doing the trick differently and attempt to catch up with you . . . you've *got 'em*!

Second, some tricks are meant to be repeated. These tricks are cleverly designed, and repeating them will not put their secret in danger of being discovered. In fact, some tricks may even *depend* on you repeating them. Don't overdo it, though. Watching the same trick over and over again, even with variations, can get boring. Plus, if you perform the trick too many times, someone may just figure it out.

Finally, certain tricks are called "sucker tricks." The magician will perform these tricks and then offer to explain their secret. She begins to perform the trick again, going through it step by step—and ends up fooling the audience once again! The audience then realizes the magician was never really revealing the secret at all—it was all part of the trick!

CATEGORIES OF MAGIC

There are many, many magic tricks. And new ones are developed every day! However many there are, all the tricks you will see performed, all the tricks you will read about in this and other books, all the tricks you will buy in magic stores—*all* of them fall into one of ten categories. Many times a trick will fall under more than one category, but all will always fall into at least one. The categories are

- *Levitation*—This is a trick whereby the magician causes something or someone to float in midair without any visible means of support. The Floating Lady and David Copperfield's Flying are **levitation** tricks.

- *Penetration*—Two solid objects appear to pass through each other without either being damaged in the process. Houdini, and many magicians since, performed a trick called Walking Through a Wall. As the title describes, the magician walks through an apparently solid wall. The Chinese Linking Rings is another example of a **penetration** trick.

- *Production*—The sudden appearance of an object or person. Magicians very often make birds, cards, handkerchiefs, coins, and a variety of other objects appear at their fingertips.

- *Restoration*—The magician destroys something, such as tearing a strip of paper into pieces or cutting a rope in half, and then magically puts it back together again.

- *Suspension*—This is similar to a levitation trick, with one difference. During a levitation trick, the audience cannot see any support whatsoever. In a **suspension** trick, however, a means of support is visible, though it's operating in an impossible manner. For example: Imagine that two chairs are positioned on stage, back to back, about five feet apart. An assistant is placed on these chairs so she is lying across the tops of them. The back of one chair is resting under her neck, while the other is positioned under her ankles. The magician removes the chair from under her ankles, yet the woman magically stays horizontal. Only the chair under her neck is supporting her—*nothing else*!

- *Transformation*—An object or person appears to change into something or someone else.

- *Transposition*—An object or person switches places with something or someone else, or the object or person magically transports from one location to another.

- *Vanish*—This is the opposite of a **production** trick. Here, objects or people disappear into thin air.

- *Extrasensory Perception (ESP)*—While some may consider this a completely separate form of magic, it is included here by way of introduction. Tricks of this type are also called "mentalism" tricks because they deal with the mind and "mind reading." Not surprisingly, magicians who perform these types of tricks sometimes call themselves "mentalists." You will be learning some mentalism tricks in this book.

- *Betcha*—This type of trick involves a stunt or puzzle the magician can perform but a **spectator** attempts and fails. Tricks of this kind are called "betchas" (that is, "I bet you . . .").

Another form of magic is an entirely different branch of the art. These tricks, sometimes called "escapes," are more like physical feats than like typical magic tricks. Harry Houdini made this style of magic very popular in the first part of the 20th century. Houdini escaped from ropes, chains, handcuffs, locked trunks dropped into rivers, straitjackets while hanging upside down, even locked jail cells—sometimes unlocking other cells in the jail and switching the prisoners around before locking them up again.

KIDSOURCE TIPS

Do not, for any reason, try an escape trick without knowing exactly what you are doing and preparing yourself properly to pull it off. Feats of escape generally take years of practice and physical conditioning to perform successfully. Also, many of the escapes are dangerous to perform. The escape tricks described in this book, while they do take practice, are not as physically demanding as most. Nor are they as dangerous as hanging upside down in a straitjacket. Leave that kind of feat to the pros!

Houdini and the Legendary Lunch

There is a story about Harry Houdini that may be more legend than fact. But either way, it's a good story. The story goes that Houdini had a reputation for not paying his fair share of the bill when dining in a restaurant with other performers. A magician named Meyenberg decided he would change that. One day after finishing lunch with Houdini and some other vaudeville performers, Meyenberg asked Houdini if he would like to see a new trick Meyenberg had been working on. Houdini said, "Sure." So Meyenberg instructed him to put both of his hands flat on the table, his palms facing down. Meyenberg next placed two full glasses of water on the backs of Houdini's hands, one on each hand. Meyenberg then smiled and said, "Let's see you get out of that without paying the bill!" as he and the other performers left the table.

A Brief Word About Patter

Patter is a term used by magicians to describe the words they say while they are performing a trick. Patter, then, is basically a magic trick's script, a means to take the audience from the beginning of a trick to the end. It can be used to set the mood for a trick or to help the trick seem more magical.

Two Magic Words You Should Know

Two words that will be used throughout this book are *effect* and *method*. Expect to see them frequently, too, as you read more about magic. You will also come across them in the instructions to most tricks bought in a magic shop.

Effect is the trick itself. In other words, whenever you are performing a magic trick, you are performing a magic effect. *Effect* can be thought of as "what the audience sees."

Method is the secret of the magic trick. It is the way of accomplishing the effect. Get it?

The Magician's Most Powerful Tool

The most important tool a magician has cannot be bought in a magic shop. It isn't a prop you can make yourself, and with any luck, it is something your audience will never see.

It is called **"misdirection."**

Misdirection is the practice of diverting the eyes, and therefore the minds, of your spectators. You will find there are people who believe the old saying "The hand is quicker than the eye." The hand is not quicker than the eye. It is virtually impossible for anyone to move his or her hand faster than detected by the human eye. The first person to say "The hand is quicker than the eye" was probably fooled by misdirection!

Magicians use misdirection whenever they don't want you to see the secret to the trick being performed. This can be done in many different ways. The most powerful way is with the eyes.

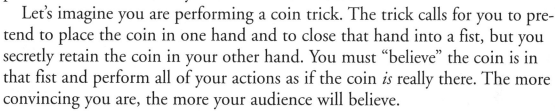

Remember this statement for as long as you perform magic: The audience will look wherever you look. In order to focus your audience's attention in a certain direction—whether you're performing for one person or one hundred people—you must focus your attention in that same direction. Do not look where the action is taking place, only where the action is *supposed* to be taking place. That is then where your audience will look.

Let's imagine you are performing a coin trick. The trick calls for you to pretend to place the coin in one hand and to close that hand into a fist, but you secretly retain the coin in your other hand. You must "believe" the coin is in that fist and perform all of your actions as if the coin *is* really there. The more convincing you are, the more your audience will believe.

The success of misdirection also depends on keeping your actions as normal and unaffected as possible. No one is going to believe you really put that coin in your hand if you seem to place it there awkwardly. No extra moves either! To be convincing, you must act as if what you are doing is completely natural.

Here is an idea to help you practice this. Study how your hands move and interact with each other when you *really* place the coin into your fist with your opposite fingers. Look carefully at every movement each hand makes. What do you see? Now make it look that exact same way when you *pretend* to place the coin into your hand, while secretly retaining it in the other. The more you can make your actions look normal, the more amazing your trick will appear.

Another way of misdirecting your audience is to condition them, through repetition, to accept your actions as natural. Let's use the example of the coin trick again to demonstrate. You show the coin in one hand, then place it in the other, closing that hand into a fist. You announce that you will make the coin **vanish**. You blow on the fist and then open it. The audience sees the coin is still there. You seem confused, and pick up the coin. You then realize you "forgot to say the magic words." You offer to do the trick again and appear to place the coin back into your hand, but this time you secretly retain it. As if it contained the coin, your hand closes into a fist, just as before. If you make these actions look exactly the same as the first time when you *really* placed the coin into your hand, no one should suspect anything. You then focus your attention on the fist—*more* misdirection. You say a magic word and blow on your fist. Next you open the fist to show that the coin has "vanished."

In this example, you conditioned your audience by repeating your actions and making them look the same each time—even though they were, in fact, different. Because the first time out you really did place the coin into your hand, the audience accepted the transfer as normal. When you then *pretended* to place the coin back into that hand, the audience believed you really put it there because your actions *looked the same as before.*

An additional technique recruits a spectator in your misdirection. For example, in that same coin trick, once the coin was "in" your fist, you could ask a spectator to blow on it to make the coin vanish. All of his attention will be on performing that action (as will the attention of the rest of the audience). This will give you ample time to slip the coin (there for real in your other hand) into a pocket. All of the attention, including yours, is directed away from this secret move, and it therefore stays secret.

Knowing your spectator's name can be a very powerful verbal misdirection tool. People are in the habit of looking when they hear their name. Use this to your advantage. Let's say you are having a particularly tough time directing a spectator's attention using any of the techniques already described. Pause a moment; then slip their name into your patter and see if they don't look you right in the eyes! This will give you all the time you need to slip that secretly hidden coin into a pocket.

PRACTICE, PRACTICE, PRACTICE!

The old phrase "Practice makes perfect" is especially true in magic. The more you practice a trick, the better you will perform it. Practice is not something to be taken lightly. Anyone can go to a magic shop, buy a trick, get it home, tear it open, and just do it. However the results will be less than satisfying—for both the audience *and* the performer. A trick must be practiced for the audience to believe it. The true art of magic is not how to do the trick, but the *effect* you create in the audience's mind when you perform it.

Always practice even the simplest of tricks. Some tricks you buy may be labeled: "No practice required" or "Trick is self-working. Perform in two minutes." Don't believe it. No tricks are truly "self-working." *You* must perform *some* sort of action to get this "self-working" trick to work. If nothing else, you must practice it until you have the order of steps down pat. If you leave out or forget a step, the trick might *not* work.

Some tricks require a **gimmick,** or a "secret" piece of some sort. The Vanishing Paper Clip on page 33 is an example of a trick using a gimmick. Never neglect practice on tricks with gimmicks. The gimmick is there to *enhance* the overall effect on your audience rather than to make the trick easier. Sometimes you will need to hide the gimmick after the trick so your audience can't see it. Guess what? More practice!

If the trick calls for special clothing (you might need to be wearing long sleeves, for example), make sure you wear that clothing when practicing. Everything the trick requires must be included in your practice sessions. Don't think to yourself, for example, *Well, I haven't found a box big enough for this trick yet, but I have everything else. I'll just practice without the box and get one later. The box isn't that important to the trick anyway.* It doesn't matter how small a role a prop plays, you must wait to rehearse until you find it. Something might occur while rehearsing with the prop that you never expected. Better it happens first in rehearsal than in front of an audience! Practice with *all* of your props and work out the bugs in rehearsal.

You'll want to practice one trick at a time. Don't try to learn a bunch of new tricks all at once. The more you focus on one trick, the more you will be

KIDSOURCE TIPS

A good place to practice your magic is in front of a mirror. A mirror will show you the trick from the *audience's* point of view. That is, when you look into the mirror, you are watching yourself perform the trick in the same way your audience will be watching you perform it. If you see something in the mirror you *shouldn't* be seeing, chances are that if you were in front of an audience at that moment, your audience would have seen the same thing.

able to master the ins and outs of performing it. You will be able to discover which elements of the trick cause it to seem magical to your audience and also what you might do to enhance those elements.

Finally, practice all of your tricks until they become effortless. Rehearse them until you can do them in your sleep!

THE IMPORTANCE OF BEING ORIGINAL

Last but in no way least, be original when performing a magic trick. Not all, but many, of the tricks taught in this book include some patter. Just because the magician in the write-up of the trick is saying these things does *not* mean *you* must. The only thing you must pay attention to when studying the trick is how it is done and what you must practice in order to do it. The way *you* present the trick to your audiences is entirely up to you. You must make the trick fit your personality and *your* performance character. Imagination is the key here.

Simply stated, make each trick your own.

If you don't feel comfortable thinking up an alternate way of presenting the trick, feel free to present it as described in the book. Over time, expect to discover things you want to change. Begin making those changes. After you have tinkered with a few presentations, original thinking will come much easier to you.

KIDSOURCE TIPS

Another way to practice is to videotape yourself. If you have access to a video camera, set it up so that it's aimed at your table. Videotaping yourself is a better method than the mirror because you don't have to be constantly looking back and forth from your hands to the mirror. Also, with videotape, you have the ability to view problem spots over and over again to help you identify exactly where the problem lies and how you might fix it.

THE MICROMIRACLES OF CLOSE-UP MAGIC

"That's what there should be in every work of art—feeling."
—Dai Vernon (1894–1992), close-up magician and innovator

The term *close-up magic* refers to a style of magic designed to be in proximity to an audience—sometimes right in a spectator's hands! Close-up magic tends to amaze onlookers more than big illusions because it's happening under their noses. Close-up magic offers audiences an "up close and personal" experience, and learning to perform this type of magic can be very satisfying.

Close-up magic can be traced back to ancient Greece and Rome, though the ancestors of today's sleight of hand artists are really the street performers of the Middle Ages. These entertainers not only performed magic but also juggled, sang, and danced. Many wore bright or unusual costumes to attract attention and gain a crowd. Their magic props were often carried in small bags or baskets worn around their waists.

Today, most props used in close-up magic can be carried in your pockets. Decks of cards, balls, rubber bands, string, coins: all are potential close-up magic props.

Close-up magic can be performed in a variety of locations. Because it does not require special lighting or a big stage, it can be performed at restaurant tables, outdoor festivals, or even a friend's house. Be prepared to perform some close-up tricks at a moment's notice!

Close-up magic is just right for a beginning magician. It introduces you to many of the standard techniques all magicians should know. It is important to remember, however, when putting together a close-up magic show to include a variety of tricks. For example, don't do just coin tricks or just card tricks.

Many of today's top stage magicians can, and still do on occasion, perform close-up tricks. It is a style of magic you will most likely always perform throughout your magic career.

CLOSE -UP TRICK
BiTE BACK!
TRICK CATEGORY: Restoration

EFFECT:

You and a friend are about to eat hot dogs. Your dog is prepared exactly the way you like them, and you can't wait to dig in. You take the first bite of yours and comment how you love hot dogs. You go for your second bite when you suddenly realize your *first* bite has magically reappeared. Your hot dog is *whole again*! At this rate, you'll never run out!

METHOD:

The secret to this trick is a little preparation. You will also need to have a grown-up cook the hot dogs for you.

MATERIALS:

- hot dog bun
- condiments of your choice
- cooked hot dog
- end piece of another cooked hot dog (The length of this piece will vary depending on the length of the bun you are using; experiment with different lengths until you find the right one.)
- table

TO PREPARE:

1. Prepare your bun by putting a condiment like mustard or ketchup on it. Do not spread this condiment on the bun. Instead, glop it there

with a knife or squirt it directly on the bun from the container. It should cover the entire length of the bun.

2. Position the hot dog in the bun so that one end sticks out farther than normal.

3. Place the hot dog end piece into the bun so the flat (cutoff) side touches the round end of the dog that's whole. This end piece will now extend from the end of the bun. (Looking at this from the side, you should see a single hot dog in a bun.)

4. Place condiments all along the top of the dog and the end piece, making sure to completely cover, so as to hide, the place where the dog and piece meet. It is important, however, that you remember where that place is.

TO PERFORM:

1. Hold the hot dog bun in position to take a bite with the end piece pointing toward your mouth. While holding the bun, place the index finger of the hand farthest away from you on the far end of the hot dog (the one that's whole).

2. Take a bite, making sure that you take the end piece only into your mouth. As you begin to chew, bring your hands, still holding the hot dog in the same position, down to the table.

3. As you chew, push the far end of the hot dog with your index finger. The condiments on the bun should help the dog slide through until its other end protrudes from the bitten-off part of the bun. After you swallow the first bite, go for your second one. Stop and stare at the hot dog. It has magically restored itself!

CLOSE-UP TRICK

COIN COMING THROUGH!

TRICK CATEGORY: Penetration

EFFECT:

A coin magically penetrates a handkerchief.

METHOD:

The coin is really on the outside of the handkerchief, though it appears to your audience that it is covered up.

MATERIALS:

- coin
- handkerchief

Both of these items may be borrowed from members of your audience during the performance of the trick, but be sure to have a coin and handkerchief of your own on hand just in case.

TO PERFORM:

1. Begin by holding the coin by the edge vertically with your fingers and thumb (your right if you're right-handed, left if you're left-handed).

2. With your other hand, cover the coin with the handkerchief. Make sure the handkerchief hangs down evenly on all sides. The coin should be positioned in the center of the handkerchief.

HAND HOLDING COIN
UNDER HANDKERCHIEF

3. As you are adjusting the cloth into this position, the thumb holding the coin pinches a small bit of fabric between the thumb and coin and holds it in place. Keep a firm grip on this bit of material!

PINCH
COIN

4. Once the handkerchief is in place, offer to show your audience the coin one last time. "Nothing sneaky has occurred . . . *yet!*" you say as you begin to uncover the coin. You do this by pulling the front half of the handkerchief (the part facing the audience) back toward you, uncovering the coin. (You will only be able to pull the handkerchief back so far because of the fabric pinched behind the coin.) Let the handkerchief, now folded in half, lay across your arm.

5. Allow the audience to see the coin; then cover it back up. But instead of simply moving the front half of the handkerchief back into position, pick up *both* halves and move them together over the coin. Let both halves then hang down in front of your hand. Although it will look to your audience as if you have covered the coin, you have secretly folded the cloth in half so your coin is no longer covered. Instead, it is being held against the back of the handkerchief by your thumb.

PINCH — COIN

PERFORMER'S
VIEW

6. Grab the coin "through" the handkerchief from the top with your free fingers. Your thumb is placed directly on the coin. Your other hand lets go of its grip on the coin and is now free to wrap the coin in the handkerchief. Do this by folding the right side of the handkerchief to the left and the left side of the handkerchief to the right, crossing over the first fold you made. The coin should now be hidden from view and the folds held in place with your thumb.

COIN

SECOND →
WRAP

FIRST
WRAP

7. The fingers of the hand that did the wrapping now grip the wrapped coin as your opposite hand lets go of it and slides down below, grasping the excess fabric in a fist. The hand gripping the coin twists it one full turn, twisting the fabric with it, then stops.

8. Ask a spectator to wave her hand over the handkerchief and coin. "That magically softens the handkerchief so the coin can pass through," you tell her.

9. Once the spectator has made her "magic wave," you begin to unwrap the coin with the fingers and thumb of the hand holding it, while the other hand does not move from its fist position. As you pull the fabric away from the coin, it will appear as if the coin is penetrating the cloth.

10. Once the coin has fully emerged, shake out the handkerchief to show that it is still in one piece!

CLOSE-UP TRICK
FLIPPIN' CUPS!
TRICK CATEGORY: Betcha

EFFECT:

In this magic puzzle, you turn three cups in a certain way, and no matter how simple your actions seem or how hard they try, your volunteers cannot duplicate them.

METHOD:

A volunteer cannot duplicate the stunt because you start with the cups in a different position than your volunteer does. The difference is so subtle, however, that the volunteer doesn't notice.

MATERIALS:

• three drinking cups

These can be any size, though all three should be of equal size. Also, the smaller they are, the easier they are to handle.

TO PERFORM:

1. Set up the cups, from left to right, in a line in front of you. They must be placed a particular way. The left cup (cup #1) is placed mouth up, the middle cup (cup #2) is placed mouth down, and the right cup (cup #3) is placed mouth up. *Do not bring attention to the way the cups are placed!*

2. Face your audience and say, "I bet I can get all three of these cups mouth down in three moves by turning only two cups on each move."

3. You begin turning over cups, end for end, two with each move. You must turn them in the following order:

   • Turn over cups #1 and #2.

   • Turn over cups #1 and #3.

   • Again turn over cups #1 and #2.

   All three cups should now be mouth down.

4. Ask for a volunteer to duplicate your actions.

5. When someone volunteers, set up the cups for him by flipping the middle cup mouth up and leaving the two outside cups mouth down. Your volunteer and audience don't realize it, but this is *exactly opposite* from the way *you* started. If your volunteer follows your movements exactly from this starting point, he or she will end up with all three cups *mouth up*!

29

KIDSOURCE TIPS

It is critical that your audience's attention is drawn away from the way the cups are set up at the beginning. Try distracting them by talking to them. Say something like "How good are all of you at figuring out puzzles? This one is very simple, but most people still seem to have trouble with it." By the time you finish this sentence, the cups should be set up and ready to go. Also, maintaining eye contact with your audience as you talk with them will keep their attention at eye level and away from the cups.

CLOSE-UP TRICK
RATTLE MONTE
TRICK CATEGORY: Betcha

 ## EFFECT:

Three index cards, rolled into tubes and sealed at both ends, are laid out on a table. The performer picks up and shakes all three in turn. One rattles while the other two do not. The magician mixes all three tubes up, then asks a volunteer to pick the one that rattles. The volunteer makes a guess but is wrong—repeatedly.

 ## METHOD:

This trick is accomplished by another tube, hidden out of sight. This "secret" tube is the one that rattles.

MATERIALS:

• four 3" × 5" index cards
• clear adhesive tape

- scissors
- a few grains of uncooked rice, some BBs, or anything else small enough to freely roll around in one of the tubes and make it rattle
- table

TO PREPARE:

You must first make the tubes, including the one that's the "gimmick."

1. Roll all of the index cards, from short end to short end, into tubes. Tape them to stay in that rolled position.

2. Pinch or fold the ends of three of the tubes closed, and tape them shut.

3. Do the same to *one end* of the remaining tube, leaving the other end open. Put the rice, or whatever you are using to create the rattling sound, into the open end of the tube.

4. Now, using the scissors, cut this tube in half and trim it down to a size that can easily be hidden in your hand. Then tape the open end closed. This short rattling tube—the "gimmick" —is the secret to the whole trick.

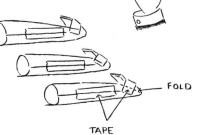

TO PERFORM:

1. You must be sitting at a table. The short rattling tube, or "gimmick," is hidden in your lap. The three long tubes are laid out in a line on the table.

2. Tell your audience that two of the tubes are empty. Pick up the one on the right with your right index finger and thumb. The rest of the hand should be curled in a fist. Shake the tube.

3. Put it down and pick up the tube on the left with your left index finger and thumb. Now shake it. At the same time, your free hand casually drops into your lap and picks up the gimmick. The hand curls into a fist around the gimmick, keeping it hidden.

GIMMICK

4. Once the second tube has been shaken and placed back on the table, the index finger and thumb of the hand secretly holding the gimmick pick up the middle tube and shake it. Thanks to the gimmick hidden in your fist, it will seem as if the middle tube is rattling. Replace the middle tube and sit back, casually resting both your hands in your lap.

5. "I will mix these tubes up. See if you can keep track of the one that rattles," you say. Bring your hands back into view, leaving the gimmick in your lap, and rapidly mix the tubes around on the table.

6. Ask a volunteer to shake the one she thinks rattles. While she is deciding, drop your hands into your lap again. Pick up the gimmick and hide it again in your fist, getting ready to move that hand back into view.

7. Whichever tube your volunteer chooses will not make a sound. Offer her another chance. Her second choice won't rattle either.

8. You immediately pick up the remaining tube as before, between the index finger and thumb (with the gimmick hidden in the fist), and shake it. It will, of course, rattle. This process can be repeated over and over with your volunteer failing every time. But don't overdo it, or someone may catch on!

RATTLE HIDDEN IN HAND.

RATTLE

KIDSOURCE TIPS

It is very important that every time you pick up a tube and shake it, it is held between your index finger and thumb with the rest of the fingers curled into a fist. *It must look the same every time!* If your hand were to change positions only when shaking the "rattling one," your audience might become wise to the trick. Also, be careful when transporting the gimmick to and from your lap. Don't allow it to rattle too early!

CLOSE-UP TRICK
THE VANISHING PAPER CLIP
TRICK CATEGORY: Vanish

EFFECT:

A single paper clip is placed alone on a table. With a mystical wave of your hands, you cause the clip to vanish!

METHOD:

This trick can look very spooky if practiced enough. The clip is there one moment, and then it is suddenly gone! The secret? Magnetism!

MATERIALS:

- small magnet
- paper clip
- table

Note: It is best to wear a shirt with long sleeves.

TO PREPARE: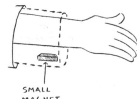

Place the magnet in your left sleeve (your right if you're left-handed), near the cuff. Try to keep the magnet in that position. (This should not be too difficult, as the sleeve tends to narrow toward the cuff.) You can even rest your hand and arm on the table during the first part of this trick to help keep the magnet in place.

SMALL MAGNET

TO PERFORM:

1. Place the paper clip on the table, directly in front of you. Allow your audience to get a good look at it.

2. Now, slowly and deliberately, wave your hands over the paper clip. Do this so the hands cross over each other. The left hand should be at the bottom while the right hand crosses over top of it and moves to the left. (Reverse this if you're left-handed.) The two hands will form an X. The bottom hand should be positioned so the magnet crosses over the clip. The magnet should never *touch* the clip. The clip will be attracted to the magnet and will therefore stick to the bottom of your sleeve.

KIDSOURCE TIPS

Be careful not to tip the arm with the magnet on the sleeve toward the audience after the clip has "vanished," or they will see it clinging to the sleeve. Keep it hidden until you can get away by yourself and remove both the magnet and clip.

Also, depending on the length of the magnet, you can do this trick without wearing a long-sleeved shirt (or with the sleeves rolled up). For example, a longer magnet can be concealed under the band of your watch.

Above all, *practice!* This trick can look *really magical* when performed properly.

3. Pause for a moment while your hands are crossed to allow the clip to be attracted to the magnet, and then slowly uncross them. The audience will see that the clip has "vanished"!

PERFORMER PROFILE: JOHNNY ACE PALMER— WORLD CHAMPION MAGICIAN

Johnny Ace Palmer is a well-respected close-up magician. Born in Warren, Ohio, in 1960, he now travels the world to present his award-winning close-up magic.

When Palmer was four years old, his dad taught him a card trick. Once Palmer mastered it and began showing it to people, "no one could figure it out, and everybody made a big fuss," he recalls. The attention he won sparked his further study of the art. "I'm glad he didn't teach me to bake a cake," Palmer says, "or I might have become a baker instead."

At nine years old, Palmer presented his first magic show. Two years later, he performed the first time for money: $5, to be exact. At age 15, he joined his first magic club and hasn't looked back since.

Every three years, the magician's equivalent of the Olympics is held. The competition is called the International Federation of Magic Societies, and its top honor the Grand Prix. The Grand Prix is awarded only when the judges deem an act worthy. In 1988, Palmer became the first close-up magician to win the Grand Prix.

Palmer's signature piece is his rendition of the Cups and Balls trick at the end of which baby chicks are found under the cups.

CLOSE-UP WITH CARDS

A surprising number of close-up magic tricks can be performed with a standard deck of playing cards. These tricks range from the very easy to the extremely difficult. Over the years, many techniques and secret moves have been developed to bamboozle the public with card tricks.

Performing some of these card tricks can be fun, and most people enjoy watching them. But there is a danger of overusing card tricks. Remember, keep a good balance of magical effects when planning your close-up performance.

DECK IDENTIFICATION

Before starting to perform card tricks, you must become familiar with a deck of cards. Here is a brief introduction.

- A full deck of cards consists of 52 different cards plus two jokers. (Some decks have only one joker or none at all.)
- There are four suits in a deck of cards: clubs, hearts, spades, and diamonds.
- Each suit contains 13 different cards. In order of value, these cards are the two, three, four, five, six, seven, eight, nine, ten, jack, queen, king, and ace (although the ace can count as *one* in some games).
- The cards with numbers on them, along with the ace, are sometimes called "spot cards." The jack, queen, and king are called either "face cards" or "court cards."

Mike and the Mashed Potatoes

Award-winning close-up magician Michael Ammar tells a story from early on in his career when he was performing close-up magic in a restaurant. He approached a table of four or five people and began performing for them. One of the women at the table refused to be fooled by anything Ammar did. She would stop him every step of the way to examine props to *her* satisfaction. She would not cooperate with Ammar at all and generally became a nuisance.

At one point, just as Ammar was finishing a trick, the table's food arrived. The woman said to him, pointing at her plate: "If you're so good, make these mashed potatoes disappear!"

Out of frustration, Ammar scooped up the potatoes with his hands, covering them for a second, then clapped his hands! The potatoes had vanished!

"There!" Ammar exclaimed. "Are you happy *now*?"

The woman was stunned, and Ammar walked away.

What the woman, and everyone else sitting at the table, *didn't* know was that Ammar had secretly put the mashed potatoes in his coat and now had a huge mess to clean up!

PERFORMER PROFILE: DAVID BLAINE— THE MYSTERIOUS MAGIC MAN

David Blaine seemed to appear from nowhere with his first television special, *David Blaine: Street Magic,* in 1997. In this special, Blaine performed close-up miracles for passersby on the streets of various major cities. He succeeded in astonishing everybody, including members of the Dallas Cowboys football team. In some cases, Blaine succeeded in spooking a few people. Once, he even floated up off of a sidewalk in front of onlookers! Blaine's bringing his magic to the masses on the streets drew major attention to the art of close-up magic.

Blaine struck again in early 1999 with his second special, *David Blaine: Magic Man.* To promote this show, David had himself buried in a clear coffin six feet underground in New York City. A 450-gallon tank of water was placed on top of the coffin. Blaine could be seen at all times.

Blaine stayed in the coffin for an entire week. During that time, passersby ventured over to look in on him. The stunt was based on an escape that Harry Houdini himself was planning at the time of his death. Fortunately, Blaine emerged safely from the ordeal.

CLOSE-UP CARD TRICK
THE HOTEL MYSTERY

TRICK CATEGORY: Transposition

EFFECT:

Using a deck of cards, you tell a story of strange occurrences at an inn.

METHOD:

Just follow the directions carefully, and leave the rest to the cards!

MATERIALS:

- deck of cards
- table

TO PREPARE:

1. From a deck of cards, remove the four kings, the four queens, the four jacks, and the four aces. If your deck has a joker in it, remove that as well. If your deck has no jokers, then any numbered card will do. The rest of the deck is not needed for the trick, so place it aside.

2. Stack the cards you have removed, from top to bottom, in the following order: The four kings, the four jacks, the four aces, and the four queens. Place this stack facedown on the table, to the side. The joker or numbered card should be placed faceup in the center of the table so your audience can see it.

TO PERFORM:

1. Begin by pointing out the joker or numbered card. "You must use your imagination for this story I am about to tell," you begin. "This card represents the innkeeper of a hotel. He owns the only inn in this particular town and he is having a very busy night. Most of his rooms are filled, thanks to a hailstorm raging outside."

2. From the stack of cards, remove the four kings and fan them out in your hands so that your audience can see them. "In through the door of the inn walk four kings," you say. "They stride up to the desk and ask the innkeeper if he has any spare rooms. The innkeeper tells them,

'You're in luck! I happen to have four rooms left.' So the kings take the last four rooms."

3. As you say that last sentence, you deal out the kings faceup in a square formation around the joker or numbered card. Start by placing the first king in the upper left-hand corner, the second king in the upper right-hand corner, the third king in the lower right-hand corner, and the final king in the lower left-hand corner. *Remember this pattern!* You will be using it throughout the trick.

4. "Well, the inn is now filled to capacity," you tell your audience. From the stack of cards, remove the next set of four, the four jacks, and fan them out toward your audience. "But before he has a chance to put up the NO VACANCY sign," you say, "in walk four jacks. "The jacks approach the innkeeper and ask for rooms. The innkeeper tells them he filled his last four rooms only moments before."

5. You say that the jacks were upset. "'You must give us a room!' they cried, 'You're the only inn for miles, and there is hail the size of golf balls out there!' Well, the innkeeper thought for a second," you continue, "and he devised a plan. He explained that if each of them did not mind *sharing* a room with each of the kings, they could all have rooms."

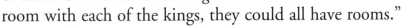

6. Begin to deal out the four jacks faceup, pairing off each jack with a king. Do this in *exactly* the same pattern as before, starting at the upper left-hand side and moving clockwise around the joker or numbered card. You do not have to match the suits of the cards (in other words, you do not have to make sure the jack of diamonds goes with the king of diamonds). Just make sure there is a jack with each king. Then remove the four aces from the pile of cards and fan them out.

7. You resume your tale. "No sooner did the jacks settle in than the door of the inn opened again, and in walked four aces. The aces went up to the front desk and asked the innkeeper for rooms. The innkeeper told them he had none. 'Don't make us go back out in that storm,' they pleaded. 'The hail is the size of softballs!'"

8. You begin to deal out the aces faceup just as before. As you do, you say, "Well, the innkeeper made the same offer to the aces, and they took him up on it. So the aces shared rooms with the kings and jacks."

9. You now remove the remaining four cards, the queens, and fan them out. "A few minutes later, in through the door walked four queens. The queens made their way to the desk and asked for rooms. The innkeeper informed them he had no vacancies but, taking pity on them, said they could share rooms with the kings, jacks, and aces. They agreed."

10. You begin to deal out the queens faceup in the same pattern. When you are finished, each corner of the square formation should contain one king, one jack, one ace, and one queen.

11. With the cards displayed this way, your story continues. "Five hours later," you say, "the innkeeper is finishing up his paperwork at his desk. Everyone is asleep and all is quiet. Suddenly he realizes that, in all of the confusion toward the end of the evening, he forgot to write down whom he put in his last four available rooms. He decides to go upstairs and peek into each of these rooms so he can be done with his work and go to bed himself."

12. Having said this, you start to scoop up the cards, starting from the upper left-hand corner and following the same pattern you have been using all along. As you scoop up each set of cards, keep them in order (that is, king, jack, ace, queen; a king should be on the top of each pile and a queen on the bottom). Each set you scoop up should be placed facedown on top of the last set, until you are holding them all together, facedown, in a stack.

13. Offer the stack to a few volunteers and have them **cut** the cards, or divide the stack, and switch the top and bottom sections. Each volunteer should cut the cards only once.

14. Once all the volunteers have had a chance to cut the cards, begin dealing the cards back out. You must deal them in the same pattern, starting in the upper left-hand corner and dealing them in a square formation around the joker, but this time deal them *facedown*. Continue dealing around the square until you run out of cards.

15. "The innkeeper opened each door and peeked inside," you say as you pick up and turn over each set of four cards, one at a time. "In one room he found all four kings, in another all four jacks, in still another all four aces, and in the final of the four rooms all four queens." Your audience will be amazed to see that the cards have magically sorted themselves out!

KIDSOURCE TIPS

The sets of cards may not always end up in the same position at the end of the trick every time you perform it. In other words, one time you turn over the first set of facedown cards to find the four aces, and the next time you may find the four kings. It all depends on how many times you have the stack of cards cut before you deal them back out. Therefore it is important to time your patter to cover the time it takes to glance at the cards in a set before identifying them for the audience.

CLOSE-UP CARD TRICK
PRESTO-REVERSO!
TRICK CATEGORY: Transposition

 ## EFFECT:

A volunteer chooses any card from the deck, then replaces it. Holding the deck behind your back, you explain that you do not need to look at the cards—you will be able to feel for the volunteer's fingerprints on the card he selected. Not only do you locate the card, but you also mark it by turning it around in the deck. You then spread out the cards and show that the selected card is the only one reversed in the deck!

 ## METHOD:

This is a very simple card trick: Your volunteer does the "dirty work" for you without even knowing it!

MATERIALS:

- deck of cards
- table

TO PREPARE:

Before the trick begins, turn the bottom card of your deck faceup and place it back on the bottom. You should now be holding a deck of cards that are all facedown except for the card on the bottom, which is faceup.

TO PERFORM:

1. Fan the cards out facedown, and ask a volunteer to choose one. Be very careful when spreading out the cards that you do not spread them apart so far that you reveal the reversed card at the bottom. It is OK to leave a few cards bunched up near the end to help cover the reversed card. No one will suspect anything if most of the cards are spread out fairly evenly.

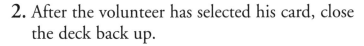

REVERSED → CARD HIDDEN HERE

2. After the volunteer has selected his card, close the deck back up.

3. Tell the volunteer to show the rest of the audience the card so they all know what it is—you, however, are not supposed to see the card.

4. While the volunteer does this, very casually turn the deck over in your hand. All of the cards will now be faceup, though the top card (formerly the bottom card) will be facedown. Thanks to that facedown top card, the deck will not appear any different once everyone's attention returns to it.

5. You now instruct your volunteer to replace his selected card, facedown so you cannot see it, somewhere in the middle of the deck. In so doing, he is unknowingly placing the card back into the deck with its face opposite the other cards!

6. You now place the deck behind your back, and say, "I will not look at the cards. Instead I will feel each card and locate yours by feeling for your fingerprints on it." What you will really

KIDSOURCE TIPS

Watch your angles when performing this trick. Be sure there is no one sitting at an awkward angle so as to see the bottom of the deck. Also, be sure there is no one sitting where they can see behind you. It's a good idea to be standing far enough back so no one can see what you're doing behind your own back!

be doing is turning the top card over. All of the cards will now be facing the same way—*except for the volunteer's selected card!* Take your time. Act as if you are really feeling for the fingerprints. Stop and ask to look at your volunteer's fingertips. Pretend that you are looking at his fingerprints and comparing what you see with what you are "feeling."

7. At last, say, "Aha! I think I've found it! I will mark this card right where it is in the deck so we can see if it is yours!" Bring the deck back in view and lay it faceup on a table. Spread out the cards so everybody can see the one facedown in the middle of the deck. Say, "That's the one! I marked it by reversing it." Have your volunteer turn it faceup, and accept your applause.

THE KEY CARD

The **key card** is a tool used by magicians to help them locate a selected card. It will look to the audience as if the selected card has been lost in the deck with no hope of ever being found, when in fact, the magician can easily locate it using a key card. As powerful a tool as it is, however, a key card is not something produced in a top-secret back room of magic shops. It is simply a card memorized by the magician before the trick.

Here's an example. The magician memorizes the bottom card of the deck (let's say it is the two of clubs). He or she then has a volunteer choose any card from the deck. The magician then divides the deck into two halves and asks the volunteer to place the selected card on the top half. When the selected card is in place, the magician places the bottom half of the deck (the half containing the key card on the bottom) on top of the selected card. That card is now in the middle of the deck, with the magician's key card *directly on top* of it. If the magician were to now start dealing the cards faceup, one by one, he or she could watch for the key card and know that the card *immediately after* is the volunteer's selected card! Simple—and sneaky, huh?

KIDSOURCE TIPS

Now that you understand the idea of the key card, here's a way of adding to the effect. Once the selected card has been placed back in the deck and the key card is in position, have the volunteer cut the cards, apparently mixing the deck up further. The odds of your volunteer cutting the deck at the *exact same position* as the key and selected cards, and separating them, are very low.

Of course there is a slim chance the cards will be cut at that position. But don't worry. Once the volunteer has finished cutting the cards, simply pick up the deck and casually glance at the bottom card. If you see your key card there, then you know the volunteer has separated it with the cut from the selected card. But in this case, the *only* place the selected card can be is on top of the deck! Now if the bottom card is *not* your key card, you know it is still together with the volunteer's card somewhere in the deck.

CLOSE-UP CARD TRICK
(USING A KEY CARD)
THE THERMO CARD LOCATION
TRICK CATEGORY: Production

EFFECT:

After a volunteer chooses a card, it is placed back into the deck. "One card in this deck is 'hotter' than the rest," you tell your volunteer, "the one you had in your hand." You then proceed to find the selected card merely by the "heat" rising from it.

METHOD:

You are easily able to find the volunteer's card by using the key card method.

MATERIALS:

- deck of cards
- table

TO PREPARE:

Memorize the bottom card of your deck. This is your key card.

TO PERFORM:

1. Ask a volunteer to select a card. As she is looking at the card, you place the rest of the deck facedown on a table.

2. Remove half the deck and place this top half on the table next to the bottom half. Ask the volunteer to place her selected card on the top half of the deck.

3. You now pick up the bottom half and place it on top of the other half, burying the selected card. You are also placing your key card directly on top of the volunteer's card.

4. The deck may be cut once or twice by the volunteer, if you wish.

5. Now turn the deck faceup and spread the cards in a line across the table. Spread them so you can see most of the faces.

6. Look at your volunteer and say, "One card is 'hotter' than the rest: the one you had in your hand." Your volunteer will probably not believe you. Offer to prove it by saying, "I won't even touch the cards. I will just move my hand above them and feel the heat rising from your card."

7. Slowly move your hand over the spread-out cards. Your hand should be open, palm down, about six inches above the cards. Run your hand up and down the line of cards as if you are feeling for heat rising from one of them. What you are actually doing is looking for your key card.

8. Once you spot it, look at the card directly to the right of it. *That* is your volunteer's card. Pull it out of the spread and announce that you have found the one card that is "hotter" than the rest!

KIDSOURCE TIPS

When running your hand over the cards, feeling for the "heat," be sure to take your time. Make it seem as if you *really* are feeling for heat. Build up the suspense. Zero in on the selected card by eliminating portions of the deck, saying "these cards are cold" or some such thing. That way, you can add some drama as well as a sense of credibility to the trick.

CLOSE-UP CARD TRICK
(USING A KEY CARD)

THE "UNKNOWN" LAW OF PHYSICS

TRICK CATEGORY: Production

EFFECT:

Using two markedly different decks of cards, you demonstrate for your audience a law of physics that was somehow omitted from the textbooks.

METHOD:

This trick makes use of a key card.

MATERIALS:

- two decks of cards with two different back designs or colors (both decks must be complete and the jokers removed)
- table

TO PERFORM:

1. "Did you ever study physics?" you ask an audience member. Regardless of his answer, you offer to demonstrate an unknown law of physics. "For some reason," you say, "this law was left out of the physics books, so many people are unfamiliar with it. The law states: When two things are done in the same manner, the result will be the same."

2. You offer to demonstrate, and place the two decks on the table, facedown. Ask the audience member (now a volunteer!) to choose one. Once he has done so, you pick up the other deck and begin to **shuffle** it. You instruct your volunteer to do the same with his deck. As you finish shuffling your deck, mentally note which card is on the bottom. Remember this card—it is your key card.

3. When your volunteer finishes shuffling, you trade decks with him, saying, "You take my deck, and I'll take yours."

4. You instruct the volunteer to fan the cards of the deck he is now holding so only he can see the faces, and then to choose a card. "Take one out of the middle somewhere, so there is no way I could see it, and be sure to remember the card," you say. "I will do the same." Remove a card from the deck, being careful not to expose its face to anyone. You *do not* memorize this card. The card you choose is unimportant. Just remember your key card.

5. Close your deck and set it facedown on a table. Tell your volunteer to do the same. Place the card you chose on top of your deck and again ask your volunteer to do the same. Cut your deck. Your volunteer cuts his. When he does so, he is placing your key card directly on top of his chosen card!

6. You trade decks with the volunteer again. You are now holding the deck you originally started with—the deck with your key card in it. Say to your volunteer, "Now go through that deck and remove the card matching the one you chose from *this* deck. When you find it, put it facedown on the table. I will do the same."

7. The two of you now hold each of your decks so the faces of the cards are toward you, and you begin to thumb through them. Your volunteer is looking for the card that matches his chosen card. You, on the other hand, are looking for your key card. When you find it, notice the card directly to the right of it. That is your volunteer's chosen card. Take this card out and place it facedown on the table.

8. Once your volunteer has placed his card on the table, you say, "All right. If this law of physics is correct, since we did everything the same we should have the same card, right?" Ask your volunteer to turn his card over. After everyone has seen it, turn your card over. The two of them match!

THE FORCE

No, this has nothing to do with *Star Wars*. In magic, the **force** is a very effective tool that should be learned by anyone beginning to perform card tricks. There are many, many different variations of the force, and it is a good idea to at least learn a few.

Simply stated, a force is a technique to make a volunteer pick a specific card while believing she is freely choosing one. This is usually a card the magician already knows the identity of. You can imagine how powerful a magic tool this can be. You already know the identity of the card to be selected *before* it is selected!

KIDSOURCE TIPS

When performing any force, it is important that your actions seem normal and ordinary. Act as if you are simply trying to get a card selected so the trick can progress. The force should *not* be perceived by your audience as part of the trick. Instead it should appear merely as a formality, so you can begin the trick once the card has been selected.

THE 10–20 FORCE

TO PREPARE:

For this force, you must memorize the card that lies 10th down from the top of the deck. Once the deck is back in its case, you are ready to begin.

TO PERFORM:

1. Toss the case onto the table and say to a volunteer, "I would like you to choose a card."

2. Instruct your volunteer to remove the deck from the case and to think of a number between 10 and 20. Once she has chosen a number, instruct her to deal that many cards into a pile, stopping when she reaches her chosen number.

3. When the volunteer stops dealing, have her put the rest of the deck aside.

4. Instruct the volunteer to add the two digits together that make up her chosen number, and then to deal that many cards from her pile. For example, if she chose the number 16, she will add 1 and 6 together: 1 + 6 = 7. She must now deal out 7 cards from her pile of 16.

5. Tell your volunteer to be sure to look at the last card dealt and to remember it. "I will be able to identify this card you have chosen," you say. Believe it or not, the card your volunteer looks at will be the card you memorized before the trick began—the original 10th card. Because of the way the math works in this particular trick, any number between 10 and 20, when its two digits are added together, will bring the volunteer back to that card. Practice a couple of times using different numbers between 10 and 20 and see for yourself!

FLIP-FLOP FORCE

TO PREPARE:

For this force, you must memorize the *top* card of the deck.

TO PERFORM:

1. Tell your volunteer that he will be freely choosing a card from the deck. "But to guarantee there is no possible way *either* of us could know beforehand the card you are about to choose, let's first mix up the cards," you say.

2. Holding the deck facedown in your left hand (your right if you're left-handed), remove about one-fourth of the cards off the top with your other hand. Turn this block of cards faceup before placing it back on top of the deck.

3. Do this again, but this time remove about half of the cards off the top. As before, turn this block faceup before putting it back on top of the deck. In doing this, you are turning facedown again the one-fourth you initially removed. This fact should not be brought to the audience's attention!

4. Look at your volunteer and say, "We've mixed up the deck a little, but let's *really* mix it up." With that, remove about three-fourths of the cards off the top and then turn that block around before placing it back on top of the deck.

5. "That may not be enough," you comment. "Let's turn the *whole deck* over, too!" You flip the entire deck over and then place it back in your hand. Look at your volunteer and say, "You must admit, these cards are pretty well mixed!" Your volunteer will agree. Actually they are *not*. If you were to spread the cards out on a table right now, you would

see that you have simply divided the deck into two halves. Half is faceup and half facedown. And the first card in the facedown section (right where the two halves meet) is the original top card: *the card you have memorized!*

6. Tell your volunteer that you will now begin to run through the cards until you come to the first facedown card. "That will be the first card that neither of us can see, and so it will be the one we will use for the trick. Does that sound fair?"

↑ FACEDOWN SECTION   ↑ FACEUP SECTION

7. Of course it does, and your volunteer will say so. Begin to thumb through the cards one at a time. You will first go through the faceup half. Stop at the first card that is facedown. "There," you say. "There's the first facedown card. Take it and remember it." You have successfully "forced" your volunteer to select the card you memorized!

CRISSCROSS FORCE

The following force can be very deceptive when performed properly, but be forewarned. If performed poorly, it will be painfully obvious! Another word of caution: If after reading the description of this force you don't think you could fool anybody with it, you are probably right! You will not fool a soul if you doubt its effectiveness. It takes confidence and a take-charge attitude to pull this force off!

TO PREPARE:

You must memorize the top card of the deck. This one will be your force card.

TO PERFORM:

1. Place the deck facedown on the table. (Your force card is the one on top.) Invite a volunteer to divide the cards anywhere she chooses and then place the top portion on the table.

2. You immediately pick up the remainder of the deck and put it on top of the portion your volunteer just cut off. Place it in a crisscross fashion so the two halves form a cross. This action must be done casually, without drawing any attention to it.

3. You must now get the volunteer to forget what she just did! You accomplish this by giving her a series of instructions. Look your volunteer right in the eye and say, "Now listen closely to my instructions. You need to do exactly as I say." This will get your volunteer's mind *on* what you are saying and *off* the deck of cards.

4. "In a moment," you begin, "you are going to look at the card you cut to. I want you to remember the card and show it to everyone here. Make sure I don't see it, though. Then, when everyone has seen the card, put it back in the deck and shuffle the cards so your card is lost in the deck." Keep looking at your volunteer as you ask, "Have you got all that? Look at the card you cut to, remember it, show it around, put it back in the deck, and shuffle the deck."

Now let's stop for a moment here and examine what is happening. You are giving your volunteer a list of tasks to perform. And, while the tasks themselves are not complex, there is quite a bit of information she must take in and process. You have made it clear that she must do exactly as you say. She therefore has the feeling that the whole trick depends on her. One mistake and she could ruin everything. You haven't actually *said* that, but that is what you've strongly suggested. So the volunteer listens very carefully to be sure she understands everything. The *last* thing on her mind right now is the way those cards on the table were cut!

5. Now for the sneaky part. Once your volunteer says she understands what she must do, you reach down and pick up the top, crisscrossed portion of the deck. With your free hand, you point to the top card of the portion remaining on the table and say to your volunteer, "Okay, look at the card you cut to." You turn your back while she does this, still holding on to the top portion of the deck.

6. Stop a moment and reread the last paragraph. If you have been following everything up to now, you will know that the card you point to— the one the volunteer picks up and looks at—is *not* the card she cut to (that is, the card in the deck just below where she divided it). It is, instead, the original top card: your force card! When the volunteer divided the deck of cards, you picked up what was left and put it on *top,* remember? Your force card, meanwhile, was the top card on the *bottom* portion.

7. If you were successful in getting your volunteer's mind off of the cards, she will pick up this card and believe she cut to it. You have successfully "forced" the card!

You must approach crisscross force with confidence. Any sign of nervousness will give you away! Your volunteer should have no reason to question anything. You should come across as in charge at all times. If you believe in what you are doing, your *audience* will, too!

Now that you have learned how to "force" members of your audience to pick the cards you want them to pick, you can reveal the identity of their "freely selected card" in any manner you choose. Below is just one example of a trick you can do using a force.

CLOSE-UP TRICK
(USING A FORCE)

THE BOOKWORM DECK

TRICK CATEGORY: Transposition

EFFECT:

A volunteer chooses a card and returns it to the deck. You snap your fingers over the deck and then spread the cards across a table. The selected card is gone! In its place is a small piece of paper with the title and page number of a book written on it. You instruct your volunteer to go open the book whose title matches the title on the paper and go to the page number also written on the paper. There he finds his missing card!

METHOD:

Use either the **10–20 FORCE** or the **CRISSCROSS FORCE** for this trick. Using the **FLIP-FLOP FORCE** there is a chance, though slim, you may expose the piece of paper too soon.

MATERIALS:

- book
- deck of cards
- card from a matching deck of cards (the back design of this deck must match that of the other deck)
- piece of paper about 2″ square
- double-stick tape

TO PREPARE:

1. Choose a book and place the extra card somewhere in the middle. Remember the page number where you placed the card.

2. On the piece of paper, write down the title of the book and also the page number where you placed the card. Put this piece of paper in the deck somewhere near the bottom. Make sure none of the paper sticks out from the sides of the deck.

3. Pull out any card from the deck and put a small piece of double-stick tape on the back of the card. Place this card carefully into your pocket or in your lap (if you'll be sitting down during the trick).

4. You must now find the card in the deck that matches the card inside the book. Once you find it, place it either on top of the deck or 10 cards down from the top (depending on what force you are planning to use).

TO PERFORM:

1. Select a volunteer and ask him to choose a card. Use the force *you've* chosen to get your volunteer to pick the card that matches the one in the book.

2. Pick up the deck and ask your volunteer to show his selected card to everyone present while your back is turned.

3. Once your back is to the audience, secretly add the card with the tape to the top of the deck, tape side up. Be careful not to expose this card to your audience when turning back around. Simply tilt your hand so the top of the deck is tilted too, slightly away from the audience.

4. Once you are facing your volunteer again, ask him to hand you the card so you cannot see what it is. Holding the deck in one hand, with

the top of the deck still tilted away from the audience, take the card in your other hand—keeping the face of it away from you at all times—and place it facedown on top of the deck. Make any adjustments needed to align the card perfectly with the rest of the deck. Place the deck on a table, and then cut it, burying the selected card somewhere in the middle. What has actually happened is that the selected card has now stuck to the back of the card with the tape.

5. Snap your fingers over the deck and spread the deck faceup on the table. Because of the double-stick tape, the selected card will not be seen. It and the card with the tape will appear as one. Your volunteer will look for his card and of course not see it.

6. Instruct him to pick up the paper, which is now visible, and read it aloud. He will read out the title and page number of a book. Look a little confused and say, "I *have* that book. It is over there on the bookshelf [or wherever]." Instruct your volunteer to open the book to the page number written on the paper. Your volunteer *and* your audience will be amazed to find the "selected card" there!

PERFORMER PROFILE: DAI VERNON— MAGIC'S "PROFESSOR"

Dai Vernon probably did more for close-up magic than any other individual. It was he who made it an art form. Many of the sleight-of-hand techniques currently used by card magicians were either invented or improved on by Vernon. He was eight years old when he read his first book on card tricks. He continued practicing his magic, eventually gaining the nickname "The Professor" by fooling many of the top magicians of his day, including Houdini. Vernon made such an impact on the art of close-up magic that many young, aspiring magicians across the United States moved from their homes to the Hollywood area to study under him. Vernon, a regular at the Magic Castle in Hollywood, became its resident magician. Dying in 1992 (at the age of 98), he continues to be respected by magicians today.

PERFORMER PROFILE: PAUL HARRIS— A WILD-AND-CRAZY MAGIC GUY

Paul Harris stormed onto the magic scene and became very popular in the 1970s with some very fresh and entertaining close-up magic. His presentations, and some of his methods, were considered offbeat. But that is just what made him stand out from other close-up magicians at the time. Instead of offering the usual fare, he performed original tricks that have since become classics. Some examples:

- A deck that has been shuffled in front of the audience suddenly turns into a solid block of cards. The cards cannot be separated!
- A selected card is found stapled to a joker in place of another joker, stapled there a moment before!
- The centers of two playing cards are torn out, making two cardboard rings. Instantly these two rings link together!

Harris's work can be found today in books, including a series he has recently produced on the art of astonishment. This three-volume set contains many of his classic creations, plus some brand-new magic. It is available through magic shops and suppliers only.

ENTER STAGE LEFT!

"I am trying to create joy with my magic."

—Doug Henning (b. 1947), professional stage magician (now retired)

Of all the magic performed for audiences, stage magic is the most familiar to people. Often it is the *only* type of magic people have ever seen, whether live in a theater or on television. Usually, mention of the word *magician* brings to mind images of a rabbit drawn from a hat, white doves appearing from nowhere, or women floating or being sliced in half. These are all effects of the stage magician.

The stage magician's tricks are much grander in scale than those of the close-up magician. That's because the close-up magician's performance area is limited to a table and the bit of space surrounding it, while the stage magician has an entire stage on which to perform his or her tricks. These large-scale tricks are often called "illusions" and the magicians performing them, "illusionists."

The way these illusions are presented to an audience varies with each performer. Some will present them as individual "bits," while others will tie them together—each one flowing naturally into the next—in a sort of magical "skit," or miniature play. These magical skits are known as "vignettes" (pronounced vin-YETS).

The stage magician's advantage of a large performance area extends backstage—to that part of the stage the audience doesn't see. At times an illusion is accomplished not solely by the magician onstage before an audience, but instead depends on the work of assistants backstage.

The stage magician also has the advantage of lights and music. Stage lighting not only helps set the mood for an illusion, but it can even aid in hiding the secret of the illusion from the audience.

Music also helps create moods for different illusions. Music can build during a very dramatic moment in a magician's act or it can add to the whimsy of a humorous trick. Used together in a creative fashion, music and lighting can greatly enhance a magician's performance.

GET TO KNOW YOUR STAGE

Stage directions can be confusing. The diagram and text below can help.

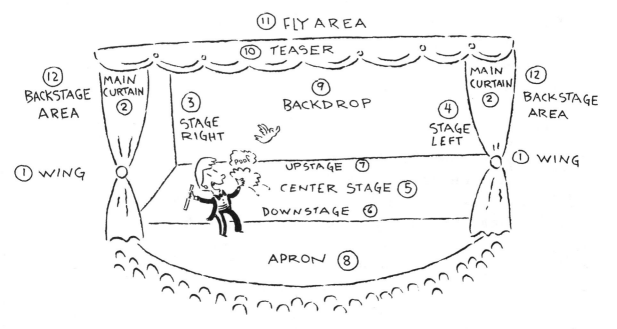

1. **Wing:** The area just offstage on either the left or right side. Performers enter and exit here.
2. **Main curtain:** The big curtain in front of the stage that can open and close at the beginning or end of a scene or magic routine.
3. **Stage right:** The area of the stage immediately to the performer's right as he or she faces the audience.
4. **Stage left:** The area of the stage immediately to the performer's left as he or she faces the audience.
5. **Center stage:** The center of the stage. The spot exactly in the center is called the "center line."
6. **Downstage:** The part of the stage closest to the audience.
7. **Upstage:** The part of the stage farthest away from the audience, just before the backdrop.
8. **Apron:** The part of the stage that remains exposed in front of the main curtain after it is closed.
9. **Backdrop:** A curtain or canvas with scenery on it behind the performer.
10. **Teaser:** The strip of curtain at the top of the stage extending from wing to wing.
11. **Fly area:** The area above the stage where scenery and curtains can be pulled after use.
12. **Backstage area:** The area beyond the wings and behind the backdrop and scenery that is never seen by the audience.

The stage pictured on page 61 is a proscenium stage. It is the most commonly used type of stage. The top of this stage is called the "proscenium arch," and the teaser runs along the arch.

Most stage magicians perform their big illusions center stage once the main curtain has opened and all of their props can be seen. Smaller tricks are usually presented in the apron area, in front of the main curtain after it has been closed. This gives the stage crew and magician's assistants time to set up the next big illusion. A stage performance must be planned out with such things in mind, from beginning to end, so there is no delay in the action and everything and everyone is on their mark.

MAGIC ON TV

When magic is presented on television, the statement is usually made that no camera tricks of any kind are being used to accomplish the illusions. For the most part, this is true. However, keep in mind that in some cases the magician does use the camera and your television screen to his or her advantage. This is especially true for illusions too big to fit on any standard stage. These illusions are usually shot on location somewhere, 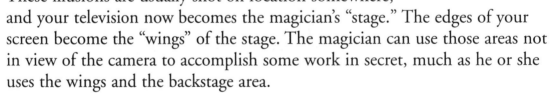 and your television now becomes the magician's "stage." The edges of your screen become the "wings" of the stage. The magician can use those areas not in view of the camera to accomplish some work in secret, much as he or she uses the wings and the backstage area.

TRAVELING MAGIC SHOWS

Live magic shows were a common occurrence in the early part of the 20th century. Magicians traveled worldwide with their lavish full-evening shows. Today, traveling magic shows are rare. David Copperfield is probably the only magician currently presenting a show that tours as much as the old-time shows.

In recent years, Las Vegas, Nevada, has become the home of lots of magic shows. Many magicians have relocated to Las Vegas because of all the opportunities there to perform magic. And, even more recently, Branson, Missouri, has begun offering "magic spectaculars" to its visitors. Magic is big in these towns, but the shows you see there rarely—if ever—travel from the hotels or casinos. It is you, the customer, who must travel. Watch your local paper, though. From time to time you may see a listing for a touring magic show that will be appearing at a civic auditorium or theater nearby. It will be worth the price of a ticket to see a live magic show.

PARLOR MAGIC

Parlor magic falls somewhere in scale between close-up and stage magic. It is a style of magic presented in a somewhat intimate atmosphere, like close-up magic, but generally allows for a larger audience. Because most parlor magic perfor- 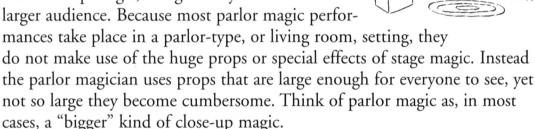 mances take place in a parlor-type, or living room, setting, they do not make use of the huge props or special effects of stage magic. Instead the parlor magician uses props that are large enough for everyone to see, yet not so large they become cumbersome. Think of parlor magic as, in most cases, a "bigger" kind of close-up magic.

STAGE TRICK
THE UNCUTTABLE PIECE OF NEWSPAPER

TRICK CATEGORY: Restoration

EFFECT:

You offer to demonstrate just how sharp your scissors are. You snip off a piece of a strip of folded newspaper. Upon opening up the paper, however, it is seen to be still in one piece. Another snip produces the same result—and another. Each time the paper is folded and cut, it is shown to be still in one piece. You finally crumple the paper into a ball and give up.

METHOD:

The newspaper you are cutting is secretly held together by rubber cement. This trick will take a bit of preparation but is well worth it.

MATERIALS:

- scissors
- page of newspaper (the classifieds work best)
- rubber cement
- talcum powder

TO PREPARE:

1. Cut off a long strip from the page of newspaper. One column of print about 12 inches long will do.

2. With the strip lying on the table in front of you, spread rubber cement horizontally along the middle. The rubber cement should cover about six inches of the width of the paper. Leave three inches on either end of the strip uncovered with cement. Let the rubber cement dry.

3. Once it is dry, sprinkle some talcum powder over the area. Carefully spread the powder so it entirely covers the rubber cement. This will keep the paper from sticking together when you fold it.

TO PERFORM:

1. Show the strip of paper to your audience. You should be holding the paper with the cement/powder side facing you. Offer to demonstrate the sharpness of your scissors. "The commercial said these scissors could cut through a tin can!" you say.

CUT
FOLD

2. Fold the strip in half toward you. Crease the fold and hold the paper so the cemented areas are touching. With the scissors, clip the fold off of the strip.

3. Now carefully unfold the strip of paper. Because of the rubber cement, the strip of paper will stick together where you made the cut. The joint where the two ends meet will be invisible to anyone sitting just a few feet away.

4. Look confused, and fold the paper in half again, exactly as before. "Maybe these scissors aren't as sharp as I thought they were," you remark. Make another cut. Open the strip again and it will still seem to be in one piece.

5. Repeat once or twice more, each time ending up with what looks like a whole piece of paper. You finally give up and crumple the paper up into a ball, saying, "I'm going to have to check the warranty on these scissors!"

KIDSOURCE TIPS

Always be careful when opening the strip after the cuts. A small amount of rubber cement is holding it together. If you open it too fast, you may break the connection and ruin the trick. Also, don't repeat the cutting process too many times. Each time you cut a piece off and open the strip, the strip will be a bit shorter than before. You also run the risk of running out of the area covered with the rubber cement. Also, you may want to experiment with the cuts you make. Try to make your cuts straight, but experiment with cutting the paper at an angle and see what happens.

RUBBER CEMENT
IS HOLDING THE TWO
HALVES TOGETHER

STAGE TRICK
SPOTS BEFORE YOUR EYES

TRICK CATEGORY: Transposition

EFFECT:

You show your audience a card with spots. Every time you turn the card around, the spots change places . . . much to everyone's amazement.

METHOD:

The spots only *appear* to change places. The trick depends on both how the spots are drawn and where you place your hands on the card.

MATERIALS:

- piece of cardboard 8½″ × 11″
- black felt marker

TO PREPARE:

On one side of the cardboard, draw five black spots of equal size, as shown. On the other side, draw two black spots also the same size, as shown. The spots should be big enough for everyone to see, but small enough to be covered completely by your hand.

FRONT SIDE　　BACK SIDE

TO PERFORM:

1. Begin holding the card up so your audience can see the five spots. (Your right hand should be positioned in the blank area of the card.) The two spots on the side facing you should be positioned at the top of the card.

2. Say to your audience, "I'm having a little trouble with this card. I'm not quite sure how many spots it has." Glance down at the card and say, "For instance, this side has six spots." Because of the position of your hand right then, your audience will assume that another spot is there, covered by your hand.

3. Grip the bottom of the card with your other hand. The fingers should be on the side of the card facing you, and the thumb on the side facing the audience. Revolve that hand 180 degrees. Once the card begins to revolve too, your first hand releases its grip. The side with the two spots should now be facing your audience.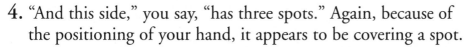

4. "And this side," you say, "has three spots." Again, because of the positioning of your hand, it appears to be covering a spot.

5. You now move your hand back to the card and grip it from the edge (the right edge if you're right-handed, left if you're left-handed). The fingers of that hand should be facing you and they should completely cover the middle spot on that edge. The hand now rotates 180 degrees, turning the card around again. As before, once one hand begins to turn, the other releases its grip on the card.

6. The side that originally faced the audience at the beginning of the trick is now facing them again. But this time, because of your hand covering a spot, it appears as if there are only four spots! Look confused and say, "This is what I'm talking about! This side now has *four* spots! What happened to the other two?"

SPOT HIDDEN UNDER FINGERS.

7. You again grip the card as you did in Step 3. This time, however, your fingers completely cover the bottom spot. Revolve the card as before. Once that side faces the audience, act exasperated and say, "And *this* side now only has one spot!" Shake your head and put the card away saying, "I just don't get it. I'll try and figure it out later . . ."

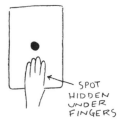

SPOT HIDDEN UNDER FINGERS

KIDSOURCE TIPS

Timing is important with this trick. You must make sure that you don't let go of the card too early when turning it to show the other side. If your audience happens to catch a flash of the blank spaces, or of the spots that were covered by your hand as the card begins to turn, the trick will be ruined. It's a good idea, then, to practice this trick in front of a mirror.

STAGE TRICK
SEALS, SHMEALS!

TRICK CATEGORY: Suspension

EFFECT:

You tell your audience you don't know what the big deal is about seals balancing balls on their noses. You grab a Ping-Pong ball and strike a dramatic pose, firmly planting your feet on the ground. You toss the ball into the air and it lands right on the tip of your nose, balancing there. You then straighten up and look at your audience. *The ball stays in place stuck to your nose!* "It's really not as difficult as it looks," you tell them, then make your exit.

METHOD:

This is actually an old clown gag, but it still plays well for laughs with an audience. Again, the secret is rubber cement.

MATERIALS:

- Ping-Pong ball
- rubber cement

TO PREPARE:

Put a dab of rubber cement on the tip of your nose, and then cover the entire ball with a thin coating of the cement. Allow to dry for several minutes.

TO PERFORM:

1. "Have you ever seen those shows where seals balance balls on the tips of their noses?" you ask your audience. "I don't see what the big deal is," you continue as you pick up the Ping-Pong ball and toss it into the air.

2. As the ball goes up, position yourself so it will hit the tip of your nose when it comes down.

3. Once the ball hits, the two surfaces covered in rubber cement will stick together, and the ball will stay there on the tip of your nose.

4. Move from side to side a bit as if you really are trying to keep the ball balanced on your nose. Then straighten up and look at your audience. They will have been surprised that you caught the ball on your nose. But when they see the ball still sticking there, they will realize it was all a gag and their surprise will turn to laughter. Say, "It's really not as difficult as it looks."

STAGE TRICK
THE SCREWY CIRCLE AND SQUARE

TRICK CATEGORY: Production

EFFECT:

You show your audience the inside and outside of a box and tube, both empty. The tube is placed back inside the box. A magical wave of your hand, and suddenly the tube is filled with all sorts of surprises!

METHOD:

This trick is accomplished by an optical illusion.

MATERIALS:

- scissors
- cardboard box approximately 8½″ high and 5¼″ across
- black paint
- brush
- items to produce from the tube
- tube, open at both ends, approximately 4¼″ in diameter
- tube, open at only one end, approximately 3½″ in diameter (round oatmeal boxes work well)
- table

TO PREPARE:

1. First cut off the top and bottom of the box.

2. Have an adult cut three slots in one side of the box. They should be evenly spaced across the side of the box and should begin and end 1½″ from the top and bottom.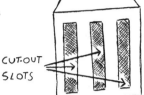

3. Paint the inside of the box black. Be sure that the paint is evenly spread and that it dries completely. You may have to apply more than one coat to get it good and black.

4. Paint the inside and outside of the smaller tube completely black, too. Apply as many coats as needed to get it as black as the inside of the box. This tube and the inside of the box must match shades of black exactly! Let dry.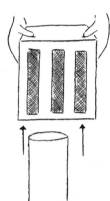

5. Once the paint is good and dry, decide on the items that you will want to "magically produce." Gather these and put them into the smaller, black tube. Tuck them into the tube so none can be seen over the edge of the tube.

6. Now put the smaller tube into the bigger tube. Put both into the box and you are ready to go!

TO PERFORM:

1. The box should be sitting on your table, the slots facing the audience. The audience should be able to see the outer tube standing upright through the slots. Pick up the box with both hands, one on either side of the box, and lift it up above the tube. Revolve the box so you are looking through it at the audience. Say, "Empty."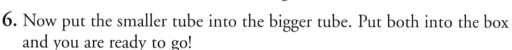

2. Place the box back down over the tube. Reach into the box and grip the outer tube and lift it out of the box. Revolve the tube, just as you did the box, and look at your audience through it as well. Say, "Empty." At this very moment, the black tube is sitting uncovered in the box. However, because it is painted the exact same color as the inside of the box, it blends right in. Nobody can tell there is a tube sitting there in the box!

3. Place the bigger, outer tube back into the box so it slips back over the smaller, black tube.

4. Make a magical gesture over the box and tube. Then reach into the tube and begin to pull out things you have "magically" produced!

PERFORMER PROFILE: JEFF MCBRIDE AND THE MEANING OF MAGIC

Jeff McBride is a stage magician whose act is always a work in progress. He has researched and dug deep into magic's roots to develop the act he presents around the globe. His performance contains bits and pieces of rituals performed by shamans, including masks and dances all for the purpose of conveying to audiences some of the meaning underlying magic. He says he doesn't want his audiences to concern themselves with *how* he does his tricks but rather *why* he is doing them: "I feel that if the audience leaves thinking, 'How did he do that?' then I have failed."

KIDSOURCE TIPS

Be careful with your lighting when performing this trick. Avoid light shining directly down on the box. This will spoil the illusion, as people will be able to see the black tube. Try to have most of the light be in front of you.

Also, you can reverse this effect and make it a vanish type of trick. You start with all the items on your table. Show the box and tube empty, and then begin to place the items into the tube. Then make your magical gesture and show the box and tube still empty. It will appear as if the items vanished into thin air!

PERFORMER PROFILE: CHRISTOPHER HART AND THAT "THING" HE DOES

Originally born in Canada, stage magician Christopher Hart grew up in Los Angeles, California, and became interested in magic after reading some magic books from his school library. Soon he visited Disneyland's magic shop and also began frequenting a neighborhood joke shop, buying tricks there, too.

You may not have seen Hart's act, but chances are you've seen his right hand. Hart, or rather Hart's hand, played the part of "Thing" in the Addams Family movies. The producers specifically chose Hart because he was a magician, and therefore his hands were very limber. He had to endure two hours each day with the film's makeup artists: They would shave his hand and arm, attach a wrist stump above his real wrist, and then apply makeup to the whole setup. Hart would interact with the actors on screen, and then computer technicians would later "erase" Hart's body from the scene.

Hart has even incorporated a routine into his act involving a mysterious disembodied hand. The hand gives Hart all kinds of trouble during the routine, and even pulls him offstage!

Hart's advice to anyone wanting to become a magician? "Study everything about it that you can, from close-up to stage. Then pick an area you like and focus on that. Don't give up. It's like learning to tie your shoe. At first you can't do it, but the more you work at it, the easier it becomes."

PERFORMER PROFILE: "HARRY THE HAT"

You may know him as Dave from the TV show *Dave's World,* or as Judge Harry Stone from the TV show *Night Court.* But before all the hit TV shows, Harry Anderson was known as "Harry the Hat."

Anderson spent his early childhood years in Chicago, where he watched con men and card hustlers dressed in suits and fedora hats swindle people out of their hard-earned cash. They taught Anderson his first few card tricks. Years later, Anderson would be in the streets himself performing his magic and playing the Three Shell Game, all for money. He was soon discovered and offered TV work. The character Anderson developed was a wise guy dressed in a suit and wearing a fedora. (Yes, that's where the nickname Harry the Hat comes from!) Anderson's magic was funny, clever, and off-the-wall. His tricks included eating a live guinea pig and shoving a large hat pin through his arm—all the while explaining to his shocked audience it was just an illusion.

In between acting assignments, Anderson continues to amaze and amuse audiences as Harry the Hat.

Whoops!

Together, the husband-and-wife team known as the Pendragons have appeared all over the world, performing some of contemporary magic's most incredible illusions. Their timing during one such illusion, The Metamorphosis, is flawless. Harry and Bess Houdini first performed this illusion in 1894. Houdini would be handcuffed and locked inside a wooden trunk. Bess then draped the trunk, and in a matter of seconds, Houdini would be seen, freed, outside the trunk. Once the trunk was opened, Bess was revealed to be handcuffed inside.

Jonathan and Charlotte Pendragon perform this illusion quicker than anybody—including Harry and Bess. Plus, once Charlotte is revealed locked inside the trunk, she is wearing a different costume!

That is, with the exception of one performance for live television in the late 1980s. Everything was going smoothly when, with much drama, Jonathan removed the shackles from the trunk and opened it up to reveal—nothing. Charlotte was in there all right, but she wasn't ready to stand up and show herself. The costume she was supposed to appear in had gotten twisted and tangled and she was not in it just yet. That night, Jonathan took his bow alone while Charlotte waved from the trunk!

The First Man to Saw a Woman in Half

A magician by the name of P. T. Selbit is responsible for inventing the illusion of sawing through a woman. His real name was Percy Thomas Tibbles. He didn't feel that the name Tibbles sounded very theatrical, so he decided to spell it backward and remove one of the *B*s. He then became P. T. Selbit, and in 1920 he created probably the most famous illusion of the 20th century: sawing through a woman. Very shortly after Selbit presented this illusion, it was copied by other magicians. In fact, the very next year, when Selbit toured America, he found that another well-known magician was already performing the trick in his show. He attempted to sue the man but lost. In the long run, that hasn't really mattered, though, since P. T. Selbit will always be remembered for creating this well-known illusion.

WHAT ARE YOU, A MIND READER?

"Ours is a game of imagination."

—Max Maven (b. 1950), professional mentalist

Mental magic, or "mentalism" as it is commonly called, is quite distinct from other branches of magic. Most mental magic tricks are of a more serious nature than other magic tricks, requiring a different attitude from the performer.

The names given to the tricks in mentalism point to the difference. Instead of being called "tricks," they are called "experiments." Why? Because the word *trick* suggests a simple stunt accomplished by a secret, concealed method.

Really, the mentalist's tricks are no different. They are basically magic tricks involving ESP. But the goal of the magician performing mental magic tricks is to create the sense that they are *not* magic tricks! The mental magician wants his or her audiences to believe the "magic" they are witnessing is accomplished through mind reading. And because, by definition, experiments aren't guaranteed to be successful, it is possible the mental magician's "experiment" will fail—especially when dealing with something as unpredictable as the human mind.

Most mentalists don't claim to have powers of ESP, though they usually don't deny it either. They leave that decision to audience members. In fact, one of the mental magician's most powerful tools is their spectators' imaginations.

Mentalism has its own categories of effects.

- *Clairvoyance*—In this effect, the mentalist appears to gain information from unknown sources. No one can see or hear where the information comes from.

- *Precognition*—The mentalist knows of an event or happening before it occurs. Predictions of some sort are generally involved.

- *Psychokinesis (PK) or Telekinesis*—The apparent ability to move objects using nothing but the power of your mind.

- *Telepathy*—The mentalist receives information from someone acting as a "transmitter." Usually the mentalist is the "receiver." However, sometimes the mentalist is the transmitter and the spectator, surprisingly, becomes the receiver.

PERFORMER PROFILE: URI GELLER— FRAUD OR FOR REAL?

Uri Geller and his amazing "mental powers" have been the subject of speculation since the 1970s. That was when Geller, who was born in Israel, burst onto the American scene. Appearing on every major talk show, Geller claimed to be able to bend keys and utensils and start stopped watches—all by using the power of his mind. Geller was tested at major universities and amazed top scientists with his apparent powers. The only problem was that magicians could duplicate everything Geller did. Therefore, many magicians consider Geller a fraud. Just because magicians can duplicate what Geller claims to do with the "power of his mind," does that mean telekinetic powers don't exist? Are Geller and people like him fakes? What do *you* think?

PERFORMER PROFILE: MAX MAVEN— MAGNIFICENT MIND MAGE

Born Phil Goldstein in New York City in 1950, Maven first became interested in magic after learning a couple of card tricks at age seven. Years later, he changed his name as well as his look to fit the profession of mentalist. Dressed all in black and wearing his hair in a widow's peak, he looks very mysterious—commanding attention merely by his appearance. When he speaks he commands even more attention! Maven's performance has been called "humorous and hair-raising at the same time" by at least one critic.

Maven is responsible for some of the most amazing mentalism effects performed today. He has astounded audiences across the globe, in person and on television. The creator of hundreds of magic tricks and mental effects, he reads over 150 books and magazines a month and has written many magic books and articles himself.

A Suspicious Subscription

Ted Annemann was a mentalist known for his clever methods and powerful presentations. He also published a magazine for magicians called *The Jinx*. Top magicians all contributed tricks to *The Jinx*.

At one point, subscribers to *The Jinx* received a renewal card. They were to send it in if they wanted to renew their subscription. The only thing was, nowhere on the card was there a place for the subscriber's name or address. In fact, the card specifically said NOT to write any names or addresses on it, just to send it back if the reader wanted to renew and everything would be taken care of. Miraculously, subscriptions continued without interruption.

No one knew how Annemann accomplished this trick. Some subscribers even compared cards to see if they could spot some difference that would clue Annemann in as to the owner of the card. They could spot no difference at all! Annemann's secret was simplicity itself. He simply renewed everybody's subscription, figuring they all would have anyway!

MENTALISM EXPERIMENT
THE CARD & HARDWARE PREDICTION

EXPERIMENT CATEGORY: Precognition

EFFECT:

You display a sealed envelope with a playing card inside. You next show the audience a small metal washer and an index card. On the index card they can see the names of various playing cards printed at random.

You move the washer around the surface of the card until a volunteer says to stop. You then ask the volunteer to look in the hole of the washer and call out the name of the card there. When you call for the envelope to be opened, the card inside is that same one!

METHOD:

The washer is the gimmick that accomplishes this trick for you.

MATERIALS:

- playing card
- envelope
- two blank 3" × 5" index cards
- magic marker or colored markers
- scissors
- metal washer
- clear adhesive tape
- table

TO PREPARE:

1. Seal the playing card inside the envelope.

2. On one of the blank index cards, write the names of different playing cards. Do this by writing the number and then drawing the suit (for example, 7♦ for the seven of diamonds). Write small enough to fit a lot of names on the card. You can do this with a magic marker or with a set of colored markers to make the cards their proper color: Hearts and diamonds are red, and spades and clubs are black. Be sure to include the name of the card you sealed in the envelope.

3. On the other index card, write the name and suit of the card in the envelope. Be sure to write it the same size as you did on the other card. Cut this out with scissors, being sure to leave a little bit of card around the edge as a border.

4. Line this piece of card up with the hole in the washer. Make sure the number and suit are not perfectly in the center but can clearly be seen through the hole. Use a small bit of tape along one edge to keep this in place. Trim the edges if needed. None of the card or tape should be seen beyond the edges of the washer.

5. The piece of tape holding the cut-out card to the washer can now act as a hinge. That is, you can fold that piece of card back away from the hole while holding the washer so you can easily hide the piece of card from sight. Do this by holding the washer vertically with your fingers on the side away from you and your thumb on the side facing you. The piece of card should be folded down and hidden behind your fingers.

CUT

7♦

FRONT

WASHER →

Front Number & Suit

BACK

WASHER

BACK OF CUT-OUT CARD WITH SUIT & NUMBER

TAPE

TO PERFORM:

1. Begin by bringing your audience's attention to the envelope with the card sealed inside. Tell them, "I have sealed a prediction inside of this envelope." Place the envelope on the table.

SIDE VIEW

FOLD

2. Hold up the washer (as described in Step 5, above) so your audience can see through the hole. At the same time, hand the index card with the playing card names to a member of the audience. Ask that person to look over the card. Using your fingers, quickly flip the piece of card into place behind the hole in the washer.

3. When the card is handed back to you, lay the washer on top of the card so the secret piece of card is between it and the washer. Keep your finger over the hole, hiding the playing card name there for now. With your finger still covering the hole, begin to slide the washer around the surface of the index card. Ask your volunteer to call out "stop" anytime she wishes.

4. Once she does so, stop moving the washer. Take your finger away from the hole and ask your volunteer to look into it and see which playing card name appears there. "If you can't read it, we'll try again," you tell her.

5. Your volunteer will look into the hole and, of course, see the name of the playing card written on the secret piece of card. However, she will think it is actually written on the index card she'd looked over!

6. Once the volunteer has called out the name of the playing card, ask another audience member to open the envelope. Take your bow as the prediction matches the card your volunteer "stopped" at.

MENTALISM EXPERIMENT
TRICKY TELEPATHY
EXPERIMENT CATEGORY: Telepathy

EFFECT:

You ask a volunteer to write down a name or draw a picture on a small piece of paper while your back is turned. Your volunteer does so. You turn back around, pick up the paper, and tear it into pieces. You toss the torn pieces into a nearby trash can and sit down at the table. You concentrate a bit and slowly identify what your volunteer wrote or drew!

METHOD:

You secretly retain, then read, a portion of the paper that contains the volunteer's writings. Practice this enough, and you will be able to "read" anybody's thoughts!

MATERIALS:

- piece of paper from 2½″ to 3″ square
- pencil or pen
- table

TO PREPARE:

In the center of the piece of paper, draw a circle from 1¼ inches to 1½ inches in diameter. Have a pencil or pen handy, and you are ready to perform this bit of "mind reading."

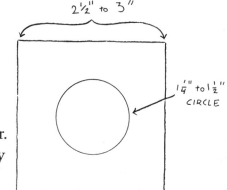

2½″ to 3″

1¼″ to 1½″ CIRCLE

TO PERFORM:

1. Put the piece of paper and pencil (or pen) on the table in front of a volunteer. "I would like you to write down the name of someone or something that is very important to you," you tell a volunteer. "A picture will also do," you say. "Just make sure to fit it within the circle here." This is to be done while your back is turned.

2. Once your volunteer announces that he is done, instruct him to fold the paper in half twice and leave it on the table. You then turn back around.

3. Take a look at the paper. It will be folded into a smaller square. Three of the four corners will consist of the edges of the paper, while one corner will be made up of folded paper. Pick up the paper so this corner is positioned at the upper right-hand side.

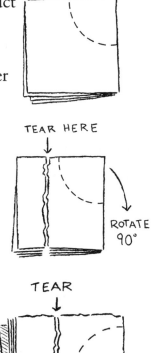

TEAR HERE

ROTATE 90°

TEAR

4. Holding the square in this position, tear the folded paper in half from top to bottom. Place the right half on top of the left half, and rotate everything 90 degrees to the right so the two halves are now horizontal.

5. Tear these pieces in half again, and again place the right half on top of the left. While all this tearing is taking place, say to your volunteer, "Concentrate on the image or words you put in the circle, and I will try to receive your thoughts."

6. You are now holding a stack of small, torn pieces of paper. Walk to the trash can to toss them away. But as you do, slide the top piece of the stack over into your fingers with your thumb. Your opposite fingers now take all the other pieces and toss them in the trash. Keep the piece of paper you've held on to hidden in your fingers as you make your way back to the table.

7. Take a seat and tell your volunteer to concentrate on what it was he wrote or drew in the circle. At the same time, you are secretly unfolding the piece of paper underneath the table. Believe it or not, this piece of paper will contain the message within the circle! Lay it faceup in your lap.

8. Begin to "concentrate," casually glancing down at your lap. You will be able to read what is written there and so be able to identify the "thoughts" you're "picking up"! Once you are done, make sure you crumple up the piece of paper and get rid of it as soon as possible.

KIDSOURCE TIPS

Do not make it obvious that you are looking down at your lap. Also, take your time in revealing the message. Rub your temples with your fingers, while at the same time lowering your head a bit to glance at the paper. If you find that you have torn the paper so part of the message is missing, slowly reveal the part that you *do* have. Act as if this is very difficult and "give up" after a while, exhausted, explaining that is all of the message you are "receiving." The more you practice, the sooner you will be able to tear the paper without tearing off part of the circle.

MENTALISM EXPERIMENT
MENTALISM BY THE BOOK
EXPERIMENT CATEGORY: Clairvoyance

EFFECT:

You display a very thick book and a stack of index cards. You then hand one of the cards to a volunteer and instruct her to insert it anywhere in the book. She does so. You return to the stack of cards, concentrate for a few moments, and then begin writing on one of the index cards. When done, you ask the volunteer to open the book to the page she marked with the card.

The book is opened and the first sentence on the page is read out loud. You hand the card you wrote on to the volunteer. You have successfully written the first sentence from the marked page!

METHOD:

Because of the clever misdirection used here, this trick will fool even the most alert onlookers.

MATERIALS:

- big book (the thicker, the better)
- stack of index cards
- pencil

TO PREPARE:

1. Open the book to a page somewhere in the middle. Memorize the first sentence.

2. Place one of the index cards into the book to mark this page. Allow the card to stick out of the top of the book a little.

TO PERFORM:

1. Choose a volunteer and hand her an index card.

2. Display the book. Be sure that the end with the index card sticking out is facing you. No one is to see this card just yet.

3. Being careful not to expose the index card on your side of the book, hold the book out with the opposite end facing your volunteer and say, "Please insert that card anywhere you like in the middle of the book." Please note that the book is never opened.

VOLUNTEER

MAGICIAN

4. Once your volunteer has inserted the card, walk back to the end of the table where the index cards and pencil are. As you do so, with your back to the audience, quickly push your volunteer's index card all the way into the book so it can no longer be seen. Then revolve the book around so that *your* card now takes its place. All of this can be done in a matter of seconds.

5. As you set the book down onto the table, nothing should look out of place. Your audience should believe that the index card now sticking out of the book is the one your volunteer inserted into it.

6. Pick up another index card from the pile and begin to concentrate as dramatically as possible. After a few seconds, quickly write the memorized sentence out on the index card.

7. Once you are done, leave the card in plain view on the table. Push the book toward your volunteer. "Open the book to the page you marked with the card," you say.

KIDSOURCE TIPS

If possible, remember details about any pictures on the page. Describing a picture or two may help the trick seem more believable.

8. Of course, your volunteer will open the book to the page marked by *your* index card. Ask her to read out loud the first sentence on the page. Once she's done, ask someone else to look at what you have written. It will match!

MENTALISM EXPERIMENT
THE POWER OF MIND OVER MATTER

EXPERIMENT CATEGORY: Telekinesis

EFFECT:

You show your audience a single piece of paper. You then crumple it up into a ball while talking to your audience about the power of **telekinesis,** or "mind over matter." You offer to demonstrate *your* telekinetic power.

You place the wadded-up paper in the middle of the table, then hold your hand above the paper and begin to "concentrate." The paper begins to move a little. As you move your hand, the paper follows it—you are causing it to move using only *the power of your mind*!

METHOD:

This can be a very startling trick when practiced and performed correctly. A magnet and metal disk actually create the movement.

MATERIALS:

- magnet
- sheet of notebook paper
- small metal disk
- table

Note: You must be wearing long sleeves for this trick.

TO PREPARE:

Place the magnet into one of your sleeves and make sure it stays put. If you want you can tape it to your wrist to make it stay, but this may not be necessary depending on the tightness of your sleeve. You may be able to wedge it into the cuff of your sleeve and have it stay nicely.

TO PERFORM:

1. Hold out the sheet of paper for everyone to see. Your thumb is on top and your fingers are beneath the paper. (You are secretly holding the metal disk in place with your fingers under the paper.) Casually show both sides of the paper while still hiding the disk.

SMALL METAL DISK

2. Crumple the paper into a ball around the metal disk. Try to keep the disk near the surface of the paper if possible.

3. Place the ball of paper in the middle of the table. The side with the disk should be near the top.

4. Now slowly bring the hand with the magnet down over the ball. Don't get too close or the ball will cling to your sleeve. Move your hand back and forth a bit while you concentrate. The ball will begin to rock back and forth. It will appear as if you are controlling the ball with your mind!

KIDSOURCE TIPS

Different magnets have different strengths. Keep in mind, too, that the magnet must fit into the sleeve of your shirt. Experiment with different sizes and varieties to see which one works best for you.

The stronger the magnet, the more the ball will move. However, if your magnet is too strong, it may cause the ball to cling to your sleeve. Therefore, you must also experiment with the distance your hand must be above the ball. Practice with different magnets and metal disks to see how far you can get your paper ball to move.

ESCAPE ESCAPADES

"Imagine yourself jammed head foremost in a Cell filled with water, your hands and feet unable to move, and your shoulders tightly lodged in this imprisonment. I believe it is the climax of all my studies and labors. Never will I be able to construct anything that will be more dangerous or difficult for me to do."

—Harry Houdini (1874–1926) on The Water Torture Cell illusion

The word ***escapology*** was first used around 1939 as a way of describing "the art or practice of escaping." Decades before, however, Harry Houdini—probably the most famous of all "escapologists"—was busy performing this art before there was a name for it. Although Houdini was a magician and toured with a traveling magic show, he became more famous for his escapes than for his traditional magic tricks. Some of these escapes he devised himself. Others were offered as challenges. *He succeeded in getting out of them all!*

There has been no one quite like Harry Houdini since his death in 1926. There have, however, been many daring escapes performed by other magicians and escape artists since Houdini's day. In 1995, magician Lance Burton re-created Houdini's Buried Alive illusion, successfully escaping from a coffinlike box that had been buried many feet below the ground.

On a 1989 television special, viewers watched anxiously as David Copperfield attempted to escape from a building that was about to be demolished. Locked and chained inside a safe, he managed to get out of the safe—and out of the building before it exploded. The next year he escaped from a flaming, floating casket before it tumbled over Niagara Falls. And in 1993, he escaped from a straitjacket while hanging upside down above a bed of sharp spikes before the rope holding him from his feet burned completely away.

In 1975 a magician by the name of Doug Henning performed a version of Houdini's Water Torture Cell illusion on live television. Henning's version had a twist to it, however. After he had been immersed upside down in the cell of water and locked inside, a curtain went up to cover the tank and the countdown began. Henning was supposed to escape within an agreed amount of time. That time came and went, and Henning was nowhere to be seen. More time went by, and viewers and crew members became more and more nervous. Even NBC, the network the special was being aired on, and the show's sponsor, Mobil Oil, had no idea what was going on.

Finally, a hooded man with an ax—who had been in plain sight the entire time—rushed to the tank to break the glass. The curtain covering the tank dropped to the stage . . . and Henning was gone! The hooded man dropped his ax, walked toward the camera, and took off his hood. It was Doug Henning!

Most, if not all, magic tricks are presented in a manner that most people understand to be an illusion. For example, while watching a magician saw someone in half, you know the person isn't really being sawed in half and that he or she will be OK. The escape, on the other hand, appears to be real. Presented in a very real environment, it can seem so real as to be dangerous.

A few performers have injured themselves and even died while trying an escape. Escapes are not to be taken lightly. They are usually carefully planned-out and rehearsed events performed by individuals physically capable of performing them. They should be performed by an experienced escape artist and not by a beginner.

The two escapes taught here are not dangerous in any way. They are presented as simply a taste of what escapes are about. Escapes using chains, handcuffs, and other such devices are much more complex and should not be attempted until they are fully understood and rehearsed.

ESCAPE TRICK
THE TIES THAT BIND

EFFECT:

You allow a member of the audience to tie your wrists tightly across your chest. The ropes are seen to be tight enough so you cannot move your arms. You step out of sight briefly and, in a matter of seconds, you are back in view and free of the restraints!

METHOD:

This innocent-looking rope tie easily deceives onlookers. Your hands are free almost immediately because of the way the ropes are tied.

MATERIALS:

• two lengths of rope, each measuring about 5′ or 5½′ long (rope about ¼″ thick is best because it is easy for a volunteer to tie)

TO PERFORM:

1. Have a volunteer tie one end of each rope to each of your wrists. The rope should be tied securely but not so tightly that it hurts your wrists.

2. Once the ropes have been tied to your wrists, cross your hands and grab the opposite ropes in each hand. In other words, your right hand grabs the left rope and your left hand grabs the right rope. In one continuous motion, bring your arms up, crossing them tightly across your chest. You are still holding the ropes in your hands.

3. Instruct your volunteer to now tie the ends of the ropes tightly behind you. "Tie them so there is no way for me to move my arms," you instruct your volunteer. Keep your arms tightly crossed while the volunteer ties the ropes.

4. Then have the volunteer step away and double-check his work. "Are all the knots tight?" you ask your volunteer. Your volunteer will confirm they are.

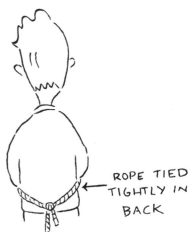

ROPE TIED TIGHTLY IN BACK

5. You must now briefly step behind a door or some other barrier that blocks you from sight. If you like, you can stay in the room and have your volunteer drape a sheet over you. Either way, you tell the audience that this must be done to hide your method of escape.

6. Once you are out of sight, simply uncross your arms and untie your wrists. Then untie the knot behind you. This should be done very quickly so you are not out of sight for long. The quicker you reappear freed, the more amazing it will seem to your audience!

7. All of this will be easy to do because of the way the ropes are tied behind you. When you crossed your arms and held on to the opposite ropes, your volunteer *thought* your arms were being tied in a crossed fashion and that the tighter the ropes were tied, the tighter your arms would be crossed. What *really* happened was that he ended up tying them so your arms could open up.

ESCAPE TRICK
ROPE ESCAPE IN A SNAP

EFFECT:

Tied around your stomach are two ropes, their ends held by two volunteers. Your audience counts to three. On three, the volunteers pull the ends of the rope, and suddenly you are standing behind the ropes, free. *You never moved a muscle, and your volunteers never let go of the ropes!*

METHOD:

This is a very simple yet surprising escape, with most of the work being done by your volunteers. You were never really tied up to begin with.

MATERIALS:

- two pieces of cotton or other soft rope, each about 5' long
- scissors
- spool of thread that matches the color of the rope

TO PREPARE:

1. Lay the two pieces of rope side by side so their ends are even.

2. Cut off a length of thread, and tie it around the middle of the ropes so they are held together.

3. Trim the ends of the thread if necessary.

THREAD

TO PERFORM:

1. Select two volunteers from your audience, and have them stand on either side of you.

2. Display the ropes in your hand. You should be holding them around the middle, hiding the thread.

3. Offer two ends to one of your volunteers, and ask her to pull on them against you, tug-of-war style, to prove their strength. You let go of the middle and grip the ends opposite your volunteer and pull against her. The thread will not be seen because it blends in with the color of the ropes.

4. Once you've demonstrated to the audience that the ropes are strong, you take the ropes from your volunteer, holding them in the middle, again covering the thread. Your hand should then drop to your side.

5. You announce to your audience that you will escape from the ropes in a snap, snapping your fingers. "Once the ropes are tied around me, I will give you a signal," you tell them. "At that moment, please count to three. Once you get to three, snap *your* fingers and I will be out of these ropes." You look at the volunteers and tell them they will be holding the ends of the ropes. Instruct them not to let go of the ends and to pull as hard as they can when the audience gets to three. "I should be out of the ropes by then," you say.

6. As you are giving all of this instruction, the hand holding the ropes lets go of one rope so the rope hangs in an upside-down U shape from the thread. Both ropes at this point will be forming upside-down U shapes and will be held together by the thread. The hand now grips the ropes again covering the joint where the Us meet.

7. This hand now moves around behind your back and positions the joint with the thread directly behind you. Once the joint is in place, each hand brings a pair of rope ends around to the front by sliding your hands along the ropes to the ends. Each volunteer is asked to hold on to one of the two ends nearest them. You tie the other two ends around your stomach. Do this carefully so as not to expose or break the thread.

8. Once these ends have been tied, you ask the volunteers to hold on to these ends as well. Each volunteer should now be holding on to two ends of rope. Be sure there is slack in the rope.

WRAP A KNOT.

9. You ask your audience to begin counting and remind your volunteers to pull on their ends of the ropes on "three." The thread will then snap and the ropes spring forward and end up in front of you while still being held by the volunteers. It will look as if they passed right through your body!

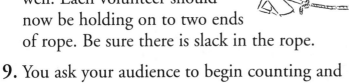

Fly the Friendly Skies, Mate!

Very few people know this, but Harry Houdini holds the record as being the first aviator in Australia. In 1910 the era of flight was just beginning. Houdini flew his plane in Australia that year, which caused the newspapers there to print headlines like HOUDINI FLIES and to run photos of him in his plane. Speculation remains, however, as to whether Houdini really was the first to fly in Australia. It was rumored that a man named Fred Custance lifted off the ground one day before Houdini. But because no photos or proof of Custance's flight exist, the record stands.

PERFORMER PROFILE: THE GREAT HOUDINI

Harry Houdini was born in 1874 in Budapest, Hungary. His real name was Ehrich Weiss. It wasn't until he and his family came to America that Ehrich became interested in magic. After reading a book on the life of French magician Jean Eugène Robert-Houdin, young Ehrich was so inspired that he began to perform magic under the name Houdini. He had added an *i* to the end of Houdin's name to show he was "like Houdin."

By 1894, Harry (as he now called himself) was performing magic professionally with his new wife and partner, Bess. His career skyrocketed, and he was seldom out of the public eye. He played all the major theaters and circuits around the world, fascinating audiences with his exploits. Houdini could apparently escape from any restraint. He even challenged the public to bring their own handcuffs, manacles, and other sorts of bonds to his shows.

Later in his career, Houdini exposed phony spirit mediums, who claimed to make ghosts appear or to communicate with dead loved ones. He would often attend seances in disguise, only to turn on the lights at the height of the "spirit activity" to catch the medium at his or her trickery.

In 1926, Houdini was touring the country with a full-evening magic show. Backstage, before one of his performances, he was talking with some visiting college students. He was demonstrating how he could withstand blows to his stomach without experiencing any pain. One student hit him before he was prepared and burst Houdini's appendix. Later, he collapsed onstage and was rushed to the hospital. Harry Houdini died one week later on October 31, which was later proclaimed National Magic Day.

GET YOUR ACT TOGETHER!

"We never find the wonderful in our magic—or in life—if we aren't willing to risk failure with the awful. I believe that to *perform* requires courage because it demands that we take risks."

—Eugene Burger (b. 1939), professional magician

You've studied all the tricks. You've practiced them over and over until you have become comfortable with them. You can do them so well you're fooling your reflection in the mirror! You've decided on the character you want to portray, and you understand the importance of misdirection.

Now what? How do you go about sharing your newfound talent with the rest of the world? What steps do you need to take to put on a show?

FIND THE RIGHT PLACE TO PERFORM

Will you be performing close-up or stage magic? This will determine *where* you perform. A close-up performance cannot be performed on a huge stage, and a stage show cannot be performed in a living room.

If you are going to perform stage magic, you'll need—you guessed it—a stage. Check around your community and see what facilities are available to you. Some theaters or other performance spaces might charge you nothing, while others may require a rental fee. Contact your local chamber of commerce for assistance.

Be aware that most theaters will likely charge you rent. However, there are other ways of presenting your talent to the public. Occasionally theaters host revue or variety shows. These shows feature different acts and usually draw on local talent. Try to get a spot in one of these shows. It may require an audition, but if you have put in the necessary practice, this should not be a problem for you.

If the thought of performing on a stage in front of a large number of people still seems scary to you, start off smaller. Probably plenty of groups in your community will welcome a free show.

FAMILY AND FRIENDS

This is an obvious place to start. You may already have shown friends and family members some of the tricks from this book. Friends and family are usually an easier audience to perform for than strangers, helping you become more confident in your performance.

CLUBS AND ORGANIZATIONS

Many nonprofit organizations are constantly looking for entertainment at their meetings and events. These groups usually have fixed budgets and cannot pay very much, if anything. A list of these organizations can be found at your local chamber of commerce. Here are a few you might consider:

Boy Scouts
Girl Scouts
Rotary
Lions Club
Elks Club
Kiwanis Club
Toastmasters Club
Moose Lodge
School PTA or PTO Groups

These clubs and organizations will have someone in charge of their entertainment. That is the person you will need to contact. The shows you will be presenting to these groups will give you valuable experience in performing in front of an audience. You will be able to discover which tricks an audience particularly enjoys and which may need more work. No matter how much you practice your tricks, you will never know how they play for an audience until you get out there and perform them for an audience.

NURSING HOMES AND HOSPITALS

You might also consider performing at a hospital or nursing home. Not only will you be working out your act, but you will also be supplying entertainment and some cheer for those who might need it. Everybody wins!

BIRTHDAY PARTIES

Birthday parties offer another opportunity for you to perfect your craft. Keep in mind, however, that these audiences will mostly consist of children ranging in age from 5 to 10 years old. Kids this age can be tougher to fool than other audiences when you are just starting out.

DESIGNING YOUR SHOW

Be sure to plan your show carefully. A lot of thought must go into the flow of your performance. There can be no dull spots or you risk losing the audience's interest. You must make your audience *want* to see what it is you have to show them. You must make them *care*.

If possible, make your first effect an especially showy one. It should be quick and eye-catching. This will grab the audience's attention and heighten their anticipation for what is to follow. If you can gain their confidence early on in your performance, you should have no problem keeping the audience right there with you for the rest of the performance. That is, if you don't hit any lulls in your presentation.

To help ensure you don't, make all your words, as well as actions, interesting. Keep your patter fluent and engaging. Make sure your instructions to volunteers are clear and to the point. Again, practice is the key. It is like being in a play: The more you practice your lines, the less chance you'll forget them and the more effectively you'll present them when performing. You may want to write a script for each trick and practice the lines as you practice the trick's moves. However, don't stay so close to the script that you leave no room for improvisation. Be ready to depart from the script if something unexpected happens. Remember, no two performances will be exactly alike!

THE PROP LIST

An important tool in designing your performance is the prop list. Once you have decided on the order you'll present your effects, you must pack for your show. A prop list is invaluable here. A prop list helps you keep track at all times of all of the props and equipment you need for a show. That is, it helps when you are setting out for the performance location, while you are setting up the show, and as you are packing up after the show to go home.

> **KIDSOURCE TIPS**
>
> A good way to plan out your show is to keep a card index file of all the tricks you do. Write the name of a trick on the top of each card. Then, one by one, list the props needed. You can even indicate the length of time it takes to perform the trick. Once your file is complete, you can pick and choose cards when planning a show. Lay them out in the order you think you may perform the tricks and study this order. You can switch around the order and experiment with different lineups until you discover the one that offers the best flow for the show.

The prop list does not have to be complicated. It can be as simple as the example provided here. You can write it out on a piece of paper, or else type it up, leaving it blank and making copies of it.

PROP LIST

Client: _____   Show Date: _____

_____   _____
_____   _____
_____   _____
_____   _____
_____   _____
_____   _____
_____   _____
_____   _____
_____   _____
_____   _____

The number of lines you put on your list will vary depending on the types of tricks you perform and the equipment needed.

To use the prop list effectively, you must list *everything* you will be taking with you to the show. This does not mean just the props such as decks of cards, coins, or the elephant you are going to make disappear. It also means any tools you may need (such as masking tape, screwdrivers, pens or pencils, etc.), a table to put your props on, and any tapes or CDs of music you may be using in the show.

A good way of listing your props is to begin with the title of the trick and then, underneath, indicate each item needed for the trick. List the tricks in the order they will appear in the show. If there is a chance you may need it, *list it!* Check out this sample prop list for help.

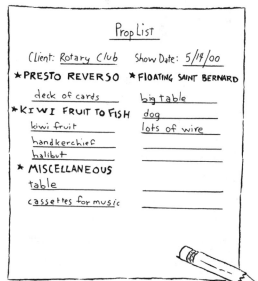

Once everything is listed, begin packing your props. You will need a case big enough to carry everything. As you put each piece of equipment into your case, check it off of your prop list. Once everything is checked off, put the list into your case and you are ready to go to your show.

Once you arrive at the theater or performance space, the prop list can help remind you of the order you will be performing your tricks. After all, the whole show is right there! You can also take this opportunity to look over the order of the show and make any last-minute changes. You are then ready to set up your show, making sure all the equipment is in place. Then put the prop list into the empty case and set it aside.

At the end of the show, the prop list will help you pack up. As you put the equipment back into your case, check each item off of the prop list, just as you did when setting up. This way you can be sure you've left nothing behind and you are going home with all of your props.

BE PUNCTUAL!

There is nothing worse than walking into a place late and seeing everybody sitting around waiting for *you* to entertain them.

Instead, get there *early*! If your show is supposed to start at 7 P.M., arrive in enough time to meet your contact person and set up your show. Remember, 7 P.M. is *show* time, not *arrival* time! If you are presenting a stage show with big effects, special lighting, and music,

KIDSOURCE TIPS

Some of the places where you'll perform may have a table you can use during your show. It is a good idea, however, to supply your own. Any kind of table will do, but it must be sturdy and easy to transport. Many magic shops sell tables that fold into a case for easy transport. Most of these cases are on wheels, making them even more convenient. If your local magic shop doesn't sell them, the shop may be able to order one for you or, at least, give you the name and number of a supplier.

you'll have to arrive in enough time to set up all of your equipment and go through cues with the people running the lights and music for the show.

If you are presenting a smaller, stand-up or parlor-type show, your setup time will probably be less. Your setup time for a close-up presentation will be even less. Even so, give yourself plenty of time. That way you won't feel rushed and stressed-out right before you have to perform. You'll be able to start off your performance with a calm and clear head. That will make a big difference in your show.

Planning to arrive early means planning, too, for travel time, taking into consideration any problems that may arise on the way. For example, if your show time is 7 P.M., and it takes you about 30 minutes to set up your show and meet with your contact person and 15 minutes to get from your house to the show's location, what time should you leave your house?

A safe answer would be 6 P.M. This gives you ample time to go over the directions with the adult who is driving, and then get from your home to the theater or performance space. Once there you can meet with the person who booked you, survey the area where you will be performing to determine how best to set up your show, and then set it up and still have some time to relax before you go on. Again, times will vary depending on the size of your show. Use common sense and plan accordingly.

By arriving early you come across as professional and responsible. It's important to provide what you have promised your client. If you are being paid for a 30-minute show, be sure that your show is *at least* 30 minutes. Some clients may not hold you to a strict time limit, so going over your agreed time may not be a problem. (This should be discussed during the planning stages of the show with the person booking you.) But if your show runs short, you may well be in trouble. Being professional means delivering what you promise, and *then* some!

KIDSOURCE TIPS

When preparing for a show, you may want to pack more tricks than you actually plan to do. That way, if you find you are running short, you can perform one or two of these tricks to fill the time. It is also a good idea to pack a small travel clock. Keep it on your table so during the show you can keep an eye on your time.

THE ONE THING THIS BOOK *CAN'T* TEACH YOU

Many beginning magicians worry about messing up a trick once they are in front of an audience. "What if, after all my practicing, a trick *still* goes wrong when I am performing it for an audience," they want to know, "what then?"

That is an important question, but there just isn't a single answer to it. Instead, the answer depends on the type of trick being performed, the performer doing the trick, and the situation the performer is in at the moment.

It is all a matter of experience. The more you get out there and perform, the more situations you will face that you have to respond to. Also, the more familiar you become with your character and the type of magic you perform, the more you will discover what works for you and what doesn't. In other words, you will gain experience.

That said, always try to bring a trick to some kind of magical conclusion—even if that means cutting a trick short, adding to it, or changing it completely. The audience will probably never know the difference. Remember, they have never seen these tricks performed by you before, so they really have no idea how they are supposed to end. Again, your job is to become as familiar with the tricks you are performing and gain as much experience performing them as possible.

DEALING WITH DIFFICULT SPECTATORS

Difficult spectators come in many different types. There are the ones who are having a good time watching the show and want to be involved somehow. They will joke with you and possibly make comments throughout your performance—comments *they* think are funny (and maybe are) but that tend to throw off your concentration and slow down the show.

Another type may go so far as to shout out things that put down you or your tricks. Chances are, these people aren't fans of magic and want everyone to know it.

Still another type refuses to be fooled. These people see every trick you do as a challenge to catch you up or figure the trick out. They feel that if they allow themselves to be "fooled" by your magic, they will look foolish or stupid.

The name commonly given to these types of spectators is "heckler." Handle them all with care. Allow those trying to "be part of the show" their comments, and try engaging them in a bit of conversation. Who knows? Maybe you will be able to use their remarks later on in the performance. In any case, showing hostility toward someone apparently enjoying the show only makes you out to be nasty and unprofessional in the audience's eyes.

Always remember, *you* are in control of your show. As best you can, ignore hecklers who insult you or your magic. They will most likely stop after not getting a response from you. It is also very possible that other audience members will ask the heckler to be quiet. If all else fails, simply stop performing. Inform the heckler that many people in the audience *do* want to watch the performance, and if he or she doesn't, there is an exit door. If you refuse to continue until the heckler leaves, watch how fast the people who *want* to see the show come to your aid!

The third type—the person taking every trick as a challenge—should be assured early on that your purpose is not to make anyone look stupid but to entertain people. The tricks you're presenting are meant to be enjoyed simply for what they are. It's still a good idea to limit this person's involvement with the show. And above all, with this kind of heckler especially, be sure you are well rehearsed.

PLACES TO GO AND PEOPLE TO SEE

"Maybe I'm not the greatest, but I *am* the best dressed."

—Carl Ballantine, professional comedic magician

The one thing to keep in mind while studying and learning about the art of magic is that the more you learn, the less you will be fooled by magicians and their tricks. The mystery of the trick is gone because it is no longer a mystery to you. That is not necessarily a bad thing, but the day will come when you are no longer watching a magician to be mystified by the trick—instead you are watching to appreciate the magician's technique.

Now that you have ventured this far into the world of magic, and learned some pretty cool tricks of your own, why not go and see how some of the *others* do it? Here's where you can go to see some very magical people.

The Magic Castle
7001 Franklin Ave.
Hollywood, CA 90028
(323) 851-3313 ☛ Web site: **http://www.magiccastle.com**

The Magic Castle is a world-famous private club for magicians. Magicians travel from around the world to perform and lecture there. Elegant dinners are served, and you have your choice of magic shows. You can choose to watch some intimate, close-up magic in the Close-up Gallery or experience bigger illusions in the Parlor of Prestidigitation or the Palace of Mystery.

Visit the Houdini Séance Room to view some of Houdini's own personal items. Other attractions are the Haunted Wine Cellar; the Hat & Hare Pub; and Irma, the invisible piano player. Call out *any* song you want to hear, and Irma will play it for you. You just can't see her do it!

The Magic Castle also houses a gigantic library on the magical and variety arts. Books on any kind of magic you'd ever want to learn about are here. Only magicians who are members are allowed in the library to study the many secrets there on the shelves.

The Magic Castle is open to members only and their guests. All visitors must be over 21 years of age. There are times, however, when those under 21 can get in. For example, during Sunday brunch, kids can visit as long as they are with a member. There is also a special day in December called Kids' Day, when children are invited in to watch magic shows and participate in activities especially for them.

If you live in or are ever visiting the Southern California area, and you are lucky enough to know a member, the Magic Castle is a place you must visit!

The Magic Castle Juniors

Fortunately, the Magic Castle offers a program designed for the young, aspiring magician. The Magic Castle Juniors organization is open to kids ages 13 to 19 who successfully pass an audition. Auditions are held only twice a year. Plus, the audition is not easy, and only a small percentage of those who try out make it into this exclusive group.

Once accepted, however, the entire world of magic can open up for you. Top-name and award-winning magicians frequently lecture at the group's meetings. Learning firsthand from a working professional is a rare—and invaluable—opportunity indeed. Also, junior group members have access to the Magic Castle's extensive library.

Meetings are held once a month, and members are expected to attend a certain amount of meetings per year. They are also expected to take part in workshops designed to help develop a trick or an entire act. In addition, they receive their own monthly newsletter.

Once a year the Magic Castle allows the juniors in the club at night. Usually the shows at the Magic Castle are performed by top names in magic from around the world. But during this particular week, called "Future Stars of Magic Week," the best of the junior members perform in the showrooms.

Once a junior member reaches the age of 21, his or her membership automatically upgrades to a regular membership, and then that member is welcome during regular evening hours.

The Magic Island
2215 Southwest Fwy.
Houston, TX 77098
(713) 526-2442 ☛ Web site: **http://www.magicpress.com/magicisland.html**

The Magic Island looks like an Egyptian pyramid sitting in the middle of Houston, Texas. Each of its three theaters offers magic shows. You can see close-up magic in either the Gallery of Ramses or Cheops Sanctum. The big stage show takes place in the Palace of Tutankhamen, the main theater. Dinner is available, and kids six years and older are allowed if accompanied by an adult.

Magicopolis
1418 4th St.
Santa Monica, CA 90401
(310) 451-2241 ☛ Web site: **http://www.magicopolis.com**

This magic spot in the Los Angeles area features two superb theaters. In the Abracadabra Theater you can see a big stage show with fancy illusions. The smaller Hocus Pocus Room offers close-up magic. Magicopolis offers shows for all ages Tuesdays through Sundays.

Wizardz Magic Dinner Theater
1000 Universal Center Dr., Ste. 217
Universal City, CA 91608
(818) 506-0066

Wizardz is a magic dinner theater in the heart of City Walk, next to Universal Studios, Hollywood. Inside you will find card readers and other psychic types. The main theater offers visitors of all ages a fine dinner as well as a stage show featuring dynamic magicians and illusions. Shows are offered seven days a week. After the show, stop by the Wizardz magic shop and pick up a few new tricks!

Le Grand David and his own Spectacular Magic Company
Cabot Street Cinema Theater
286 Cabot St.
Beverly, MA 01915
(978) 927-3677 ☛ Web site: **http://www.bevbank.com/kiosk_le_grand_david.html**

In 1977, Le Grand David and his own Spectacular Magic Company presented their first performance at the newly renovated theater. Fabulous costumes and splendid illusions help make this production live up to the *spectacular* in its name. All ages will be entertained.

Caesar's Magical Empire
Caesar's Palace
3570 Las Vegas Blvd. South
Las Vegas, NV 89109
1-800-445-4544 or
(702) 731-7333 ☛ Web site: **http://www.caesars.com/**

Caesar's Magical Empire is an entire evening's experience. As visitors enter, they are told of a "hidden city beneath Rome," a city of wizards and magic. After being guided through an underground catacomb, visitors feast on a three-course dinner hosted by a sorcerer. After dinner, guests are offered a wide variety of shows and special effects, including the Luminaria, a spectacle of sound, light, and "dancing fire." Surprises await guests, too, in "séance" rooms. All of this is topped off with a big stage show in the Sultan's Palace theater. If you ever find yourself in Las Vegas, seek out Caesar's Magical Empire (for kids five years old and up).

Monday Night Magic
Sullivan Street Playhouse
181 Sullivan St.
New York, NY 10012
(212) 615-6432 ☛ Web site: **http://newyork.citysearch.com/E/E/NYCNY/0013/23/52/**

On any given Monday night, an audience may see incredible illusions, hilarious comedy magic, and even sideshow stunts, like someone eating fire. A different stage show is presented every week. And during intermission, close-up magic is performed upstairs. Recommended for ages 12 and up.

Siegfried & Roy: Masters of the Impossible
The Mirage Hotel & Casino
3400 Las Vegas Blvd. South
Las Vegas, NV 89109
1-800-963-9634 or (702) 792-7777 ☛ Web site: **http://www.sarmoti.com/main.html**

Siegfried & Roy have become magical legends. Kids as well as adults have marveled at their show: a spectacular mix of dance, special effects, and, of course, magic. Wild animals, particularly rare white tigers, feature prominently in the show. Be sure to check out the wild animal sanctuary at the Mirage, where you can see some of the tigers up close!

Lance Burton: Master Magician
The Lance Burton Theater
The Monte Carlo Resort & Casino
3770 Las Vegas Blvd. South
Las Vegas, NV 89109
1-877-386-8224 or
(702) 730-7160 ☛ Web site: **http://www.monte-carlo.com/entertainment.html**
and **http://www.lanceburton.com**

Lance Burton is probably one of the more personable magicians performing today. His southern charm and hospitality shine through his performances. He has starred in his own magic specials on NBC and, indeed, his star is rapidly rising in the world of magic! Currently Burton hosts his own show in his own theater in Las Vegas. All ages are welcome, so if you get the chance, go see it.

The magic shows and performances listed here are by no means the only ones around. As a matter of fact, there is so much magic happening in Las Vegas, it seems you can't turn a corner there without seeing an ad for a magic show! Other cities where magic shows are popular and plentiful are Biloxi, Mississippi; Lake Tahoe, Nevada; Reno, Nevada; and Branson, Missouri.

In addition, amusement parks frequently feature magic shows. Most major parks, such as Disneyland, Disney World, and Six Flags offer magic shows year-round. Check with the park nearest you for information.

Also, no matter *where* you live, magicians probably perform in a restaurant or two there. Keep your eyes open for ads and signs, and ask around. You're bound to find a restaurant that features a magician on certain nights.

MAGIC MAGAZINES

There are a few magic periodicals to which you can subscribe. But don't look for them at your local newsstand. You can only get them by visiting a magic shop or contacting them directly. Each magazine offers tricks as well as articles on magicians, magic history, and what is currently happening on the magic scene. Plus they have many ads for tricks and magic shops. With a parent's permission, contact these addresses or Web sites for current subscription information.

Abracadabra Magazine
Goodliffe Publications
150 New Road
Bromsgrove
Worcestershire B60 2LG
England
Published weekly

MAGIC Magazine
Circulation Office
Suite 124-179
7380 S. Eastern Ave.
Las Vegas, NV 89123
Web site: **http://www.magicmagazine.com**
Published monthly

Genii Magazine
Suite 106-384
4200 Wisconsin Ave. NW
Washington, D.C. 20016
Web site: **http://www.geniimagazine.com**
Published monthly

MAGIC SHOPS AND SUPPLIERS

Listed below are a number of magic shops, dealers, and suppliers. Most offer a wide variety of choices in tricks, books, and videotapes. The majority have catalogs available for purchase and will ship to anywhere in the United States. Please note that many have a toll-free line. This is usually for *orders only*! If you have a parent's permission and decide to call some of these vendors, please do not use the toll-free line unless you are placing an order.

Brad Burt's Magic Shop
4204 Convoy St.
San Diego, CA 92111
Orders Only: 1-800-748-5759
All Other Calls: (619) 571-4749 ☞ Web site: **http://www.magicshop.com**

H & R Magic Books
3839 Liles Lane
Humble, TX 77396-4088
(281) 454-7219 ☛ Web site:
http://www.magicbookshop.com

Haines House of Cards
2514 Leslie Ave.
Norwood, OH 45212
(513) 531-6548 ☛ Web site:
**http://www.intersource.com/~jokaro/haines
.html**

Hank Lee's Magic Factory
(Mail Order Division)
P.O. Box 789
Medford, MA 02155
Orders Only: 1-800-874-7400
All Other Calls: (617) 482-8749 or
(617) 482-8750 ☛ Web site:
http://magicfact .com/index.html

Hank Lee's Magic Factory Boston Store
(Retail Store and Showroom)
112 South St.
Boston, MA 02111
(617) 482-8749

Hollywood Magic Inc.
6614 Hollywood Blvd.
Hollywood, CA 90028
(323) 464-5610

Louis Tannen Inc.
24 W. 25th St.
2nd Floor
New York, NY 10010
Orders Only: 1-800-72-MAGIC
All Other Calls: (212) 929-4500
☛ Web site: **http://www.tannenmagic.com**

U.S. Playing Card Company
P.O. Box 12126
Cincinnati, OH 45212
(513) 396-5700

MAGIC CLUBS AND ORGANIZATIONS

There are a few magic clubs and organizations that you may want to join.
Listed here is information on how to contact them.

International Brotherhood of Magicians
11137C S. Towne Square, Ste. C
St. Louis, MO 63123-7819
(314) 845-9200 ☛ Web site: **http://www.magician.org**

Members must be at least 12 years old. Those who join receive a monthly
magazine called *The Linking Ring*. There are over 300 chapters (called Rings)
worldwide.

Magical Youth International
(See information above for International Brotherhood of Magicians)
This organization is open to young magicians, ages 12–18. Potential members must have shown an interest in magic for at least a year. All members receive a quarterly newsletter, *Top Hat*.

Magic Castle Junior Society
Magic Castle
7001 Franklin Ave.
Hollywood, CA 90028
(323) 851-3313

Members must be between the ages of 12 and 19. Prospective members should live in or around the Los Angeles area as they must pass an audition and, if accepted, are expected to attend meetings and participate in workshops. Members have access to the Magic Castle library and receive a monthly newsletter called *The Magic Castle Junior News* as well as the regular members' monthly newsletter. Auditions are held twice a year.

Society of American Magicians
P.O. Box 510260
St. Louis, MO 63151
1-888-726-9644 ☛ Web site: **http://magicsam.com/join.html**

This is the oldest magical society in the world. Houdini was the society's national president until his death. Members must be at least 12 years old, if not already a member of SYM (see below). Those who join receive a monthly magic magazine called *M-U-M*. There are over 250 chapters (called assemblies) worldwide.

Society of Young Magicians
(See information above for Society of American Magicians)
Web site: **http://magicsam.com/sym.html**

This organization specifically for young people is part of the Society of American Magicians (SAM). It was founded in 1984 by members of SAM to encourage kids between the ages of 7 and 17 to take up magic as a hobby. Members receive their own newsletter called *The Magic SYMbol*. Many SAM Assemblies allow SYM members to participate in their activities.

FOR FURTHER READING

The books listed here will help you continue your study of magic. They can be bought or ordered through your local magic shop or any of the shops listed in this book. Some can even be found at your local bookstore. A number of these books contain tricks, while others are strictly about the performance of magic. Magicians consider most of them classics, and they should be studied by any serious student of magic.

Bobo, J. B. *Modern Coin Magic.* New York: Dover, 1982.

Corinda, Tony. *13 Steps to Mentalism.* Brooklyn: D. Robbins & Co., 1968.

Erdnase, S. W. *The Expert at the Card Table: Artifice, Ruse, and Subterfuge and the Card Table.* Toronto: Coles Publishing, 1980.

Fitzkee, Dariel. *Magic by Misdirection.* Pomeroy: Lee Jacobs Productions, 1975.

————. *Showmanship for Magicians.* Oakland: Magic Limited, 1945.

————. *Trick Brain.* Pomeroy: Lee Jacobs Productions, 1976.

Ganson, Lewis. *The Dai Vernon Book of Magic.* L & L Publishing, 1994.

Hilliard, John Northern. *Greater Magic.* Kaufman & Greenberg, 1994.

Hoffman, Professor. *Modern Magic: A Practical Treatise on the Art of Conjuring.* New Delhi: Sterling, 1997.

Hugard, Jean, and Frederick Braue. *The Royal Road to Card Magic.* London: Faber & Faber, 1975.

Maskelyne, Nevil, and David Devant. *Our Magic: The Art in Magic, the Theory of Magic, the Practice of Magic.* Fleming Book Company, 1946.

Sachs, Edwin. *Sleight of Hand: A Practical Manual of Legerdemain for Amateurs and Others.* New York: Dover, 1980.

Tarbell, Harlan. *Harlan Course in Magic.* 8 vols. Brooklyn: D. Robbins & Co.

Wilson, Mark, and Walter Brown Gibson. *Mark Wilson's Complete Course in Magic.* Philadelphia: Courage, 1988.

GLOSSARY

The terms listed here are commonly found in magic literature and discussions. Many are used in this book. Those that aren't are included here by way of introduction. Study these terms and you'll have a good working vocabulary in the art of magic.

black art: a technique used to hide people or things from view. This is accomplished with a combination of lighting and a black background or backdrop. The person or thing to be hidden is dressed or covered in the same black material as the background and therefore blends in with it, becoming virtually invisible. If the lighting is not correct, the item or person dressed in black will be seen. Sometimes black light is used. See The Screwy Circle and Square trick on page 70 for an example.

book test: a mentalism effect using a randomly selected book and/or page number. The information on the selected page is then correctly identified by the mentalist. The trick Mentalism by the Book on page 85 is an example.

clairvoyance: the ability to mentally gain information from an unseen source. *See also* **mentalism, P.K., precognition, telekinesis, telepathy.**

close-up magic: magic performed in an intimate setting rather than on a stage. Close-up magic happens sometimes only inches away from spectators. Close-up magic can involve a variety of props such as decks of cards, coins, pencils, or matches.

crimp: a slight bend usually applied to the corner of a playing card, allowing it or the card next to it to be easily located from within the deck.

cut: a way of mixing the order of a deck of playing cards by removing the top half of the deck and then putting the bottom half on top of that top half. *See also* **false cut.**

double lift (also known as double turnover): a technique used in card tricks to show two cards as one. The face of a card is shown to the audience while, at the same time, a different card is held hidden behind the first.

effect: the action the audience witnesses during a magic trick; what the audience sees, or the magic trick itself.

escapology: the art of escaping from restraint.

false cut: a technique used to create the illusion of cutting a deck of cards, when in reality the deck stays in exactly the same order. *See also* **cut.**

false shuffle: a technique used to create the illusion of a deck of cards being mixed by a shuffle, when in reality the cards—or block of cards—stay in the same order. *See also* **shuffle.**

force: a technique used, usually in card magic, to cause a volunteer to make a selection the magician wants to be made. The performer knows the identity of the selection beforehand.

gaff: a secret preparation done to a prop before the trick begins. The gaff, also known as a gimmick, causes the trick to work. *See also* **gimmick.**

gimmick: a secret piece or device not seen by the audience that aids in the working of a trick.

illusion: something that is not as it appears.

key card: a card in a deck of cards (usually the top or bottom card) that when placed next to a randomly chosen card assists in locating that card.

legerdemain: another term for magic or sleight of hand.

levitation: the rising or lifting of a person or object without any visible means of support.

load: a hidden object or objects the magician "magically" reveals at some point during a trick. Sometimes the magician is required to move the load from one position to another undetected. Other times the load is already in place and ready to be revealed.

location: a term pertaining to card tricks. Most card tricks tend to involve magically locating a selected card.

mentalism: the branch of magic dealing with tricks involving the mind. Mind reading and ESP tricks fall into this category. *See also* **clairvoyance, P.K., precognition, telekinesis, telepathy.**

method: how a trick is accomplished; the secret to a trick.

misdirection: the art of redirecting your audience's attention; making them look where you want them to look using either verbal or physical means.

occult: pertaining to supernatural powers and their knowledge.

palm or palming: the technique of secretly hiding something in your hand while at the same time keeping the hand in a natural-looking position. If performed properly, the hidden item is never detected.

penetration: a magic trick in which one solid object passes through another without either being destroyed in the process.

pip: another name for the suits that appear on playing cards. For example, the four of hearts would have four pips on the card.

P.K. (also known as psychokinesis): a mentalism effect dealing with moving or bending objects using only the power of your mind. *See also* **clairvoyance, mentalism, precognition, telekinesis, telepathy.**

precognition: a mentalism effect involving the mentalist already knowing the outcome of some event before it takes place. *See also* **clairvoyance, mentalism, P.K., telekinesis, telepathy.**

prestidigitation: another word for sleight of hand. A magician is sometimes called a "prestidigitator."

production: a magic trick where something seemingly appears from nowhere.

restoration: a magic effect in which something is destroyed and then "magically" put back together again.

shuffle: the technique used to mix the order of a deck of cards. *See also* **false shuffle.**

sleight of hand: another name for close-up magic, especially close-up magic with cards and coins.

spectator: one who watches a magic performance; an audience member.

stooge: a secret helper in a magic trick who usually plays the part of an audience member.

suspension: a magic effect in which a person or object is supported by a visible means of support, but that support appears to defy the laws of physics.

telekinesis: a mentalism effect dealing with moving or bending objects using only the power of the mind. *See also* **clairvoyance, mentalism, P.K., precognition, telepathy.**

telepathy: a mentalism effect in which the mentalist apparently sends or receives information to or from a spectator's mind. All telepathy effects must have a "transmitter" and a "receiver." *See also* **clairvoyance, mentalism, P.K., precognition, telekinesis.**

transformation: an effect in which a person or thing "magically" changes into another.

transposition: a magic trick in which a person or thing "magically" switches places with another, or the person or thing "magically" travels from one place to another.

vanish: a trick in which someone or something apparently disappears into thin air.

INDEX